The Western Balkans on Their Way to the EU?

Siniša Kušić/Claudia Grupe (eds.)

The Western Balkans on Their Way to the EU?

PETER LANG

Frankfurt am Main · Berlin · Bern · Bruxelles · New York · Oxford · Wien

Bibliographic Information published by the Deutsche Nationalbibliothek
The Deutsche Nationalbibliothek lists this publication in the Deutsche Nationalbibliografie; detailed bibliographic data is available in the internet at <http://www.d-nb.de>.

Cover design by
Claudia Grupe

ISBN-10: 3-631-55896-1
ISBN-13: 978-3-631-55896-6
US-ISBN: 0-8204-8739-2

© Peter Lang GmbH
Europäischer Verlag der Wissenschaften
Frankfurt am Main 2007
All rights reserved.

Printed in Germany 1 2 3 4 5   7

www.peterlang.de

Contents

List of Tables

List of Figures

Preface

When the first steps were taken towards EU cooperation in the 1950's, the number of EU-member states has risen from only six to the number of 25 in 2004 as a result of several rounds of enlargement. At present, further negotiations on the accession of potential candidate countries, amongst others the countries from the Western Balkans, being marked by violent conflicts, are being carried out. To date, only Croatia, the Former Yugoslav Republic of Macedonia and Albania have already signed a formal contractual relationship with the EU whereas Serbia, Montenegro and Bosnia and Hercegovina (BiH) have entered discussions on the Stabilization and Association process (SAP). This process offers the prospect of full integration into the EU in the long run, preconditioned that certain political and economic terms, such as the establishment of a market economy and the ability to stand the competition in the single market, are met.

As the following contributions to this book written by different experts of the region demonstrate, strategies to create the demanded competitive structures in the different countries of the Western Balkans vary, depending on the different stages of development, inherited economic structures, and the previous transition and integration process. In this context, the selected articles mainly concentrate on the actual economic development, trade performance, the attraction of foreign direct investment (FDI) and endogenous determinants of competitiveness as education and innovation in the analysed economies.

The fact that there exist significant differences between the countries in this region becomes already obvious in having a closer look at the first chapter, written by Paulina Biernacka, that focuses on Bosnia and Hercegovina, a country that was still suffering from a violent war only one decade ago. Reasons that contribute to the county's limited economic progress, such as the complicated political structure within the country, hindering the cooperation between the governmental bodies as well as the economic relations with the EU, are discussed in detail.

The analysis of the Kosovar transition and integration period in the Western Balkan region as well as the current state of the path towards the EU laid down in the article of Isa Mulaj makes clear that a possible solution to the difficulties of the Western Balkan countries should move towards political stability as a gateway of cooperation and other integration processes.

This argument underlining necessity to create stronger linkages between the individual small states of the Western Balkans through the implementation and institutional establishment of regional cooperation as a precondition for EU integration on the one hand and for the regions' economic development, stability and prosperity on the other hand finds even more support by Daniel Göler as well as by an article by us editors in the respective contributions. Potential problems resulting from more integration such as the outflow of intellectual capital, the so called "brain drain", are being discussed in detail in the contribution of Vedran Horvat.

Finally, I would like to express my special thanks to the authors who provided us with new insights and their very valuable perspectives on different Western Balkan countries and their way to the EU. Furthermore, this project would not have been realizable without the support of my colleagues at the Chair for Comparison and Transition of Economic Systems at the Johann Wolfgang Goethe University, Frankfurt. In particular, I would like to acknowledge my young colleague and economist Daniela Blessing who did a superb job in managing the conception and realization of this book.

Claudia Grupe and Siniša Kušić

Frankfurt am Main, November 2006

Chapter 1

Paulina Biernacka:

The Impact of the Bosnian State Structure on the Economic Relations between the European Union and Bosnia and Hercegovina (BiH)

1.1   BiH Internal Political Structure

Bosnia and Hercegovina constitutes an example of a country where the economic development cannot be initiated or successfully conducted without the political consensus of the government authorities. The economy and politics intertwine to an extent as probably in none of the post-communist states. Not only more than 40 years of command economy but also the footprints of the armed conflict of the 1990s contributed to the situation where barely any decision, regardless in which policy area, can be taken without political disputes. Therefore, understanding the politics is a necessity for comprehending the economic problems of this country.

The *General Framework Agreement for Peace* in Bosnia and Hercegovina was initiated on November 21st, 1995 and signed on December 14th of the same year (Pajic, 1999). It has brought an end to the armed conflict but at the same time created an extremely complicated state structure with a pronounced dominance of the ethnicity factor displayed in the territorial division of its three nationalities: Bosnians, Serbs, and Croats (Papic, 2002). The *Dayton settlement* awarded 49% of the territory to the Bosnian Serbs (Republika Srpska, RS) and 51% to the Croat/Muslim Federation (Federation of Bosnia and Hercegovina, FBiH). BiH political structure has been defined in Annex IV of the *Dayton Peace Agreement* (DPA). The decentralized entities account for much of the political power, while the efficiency of the state-level government often depends upon the cooperation of the entities.

The BiH multi-layered system of governance is based on the three constitutions that operate in the country: the constitution of the common state of Bosnia and Hercegovina and the two significantly different constitutions of the two entities. The central government consists of the Parliamentary Assembly divided into the House of Peoples and the House of Representatives, a rotating tripartite Presidency (with representatives of each nationality) and a Council of Ministers with six ministries. The political structure of the FBiH is divided into three levels:

- The entity level: two-house parliament, a president, a vice-president and a government under the prime minister;

- The canton level: each of the ten cantons with its own cantonal constitution and an assembly with a power to adopt laws;

- The municipal level: each of the municipality with its own assembly.
  In the case of the RS, there is no cantonal level. The governmental structure is as follows:

  - *The entity level:* National Assembly, a president, a vice-president, and a government under the prime minister;
  - *The municipal level:* each of the municipality with its own assembly.[1]

---

[1] For further information on the political structure of Bosnia and Hercegovina see: The official website of the Organisation for Security and Cooperation in Europe, Mission to Bosnia and Hercegovina, http://www.oscebih.org.

Figure 1.1: Political Structure of BiH

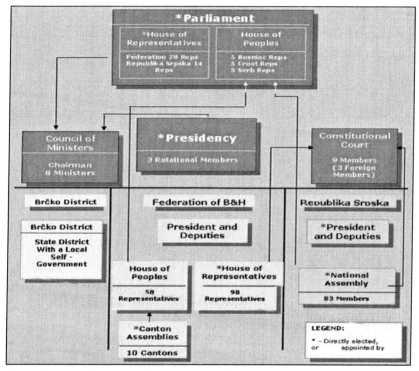

Source: Bosnia and Hercegovina Foreign Investment Promotion Agency (2004)

The real result of the cantonal division of FBiH is that the country is operating under 13 "constitutions", and close to 200 ministries. Furthermore, BiH faces the parallel existence of various different legal systems including the laws in force at time of ex-Yugoslavia, the laws from the pre-Dayton legal system, and present legislative practices of the RS and the FBiH.

The BiH internal structure can be considered as a "weak federation". Due to the low rate of entities' cooperation with each other, the central government's limited constitutional competences restrict the country's ability to fulfil the requirements of contemporary economic and social development. The duplication of institutions in BiH, complexity of multi-level of governance, excessive and very expensive administration has resulted in the lack of efficiency. As stated by the special coordinator of the Stability Pact for South Eastern Europe Erhard Busek "There is no country that has so many governments as BiH. When somebody in Sarajevo says "good morning president" everybody turns out in the street" (Busek, 2003).

1.2   BiH Recent Economic Performance and its Role in the Regional and the EU Market[2]

One of the greatest obstacles to the economic recovery in BiH, apart from the remnants of the former socially planned economic system, are devastation caused by the war and political disputes. The major consequence of the 1992-95 war, besides the destruction of BiH's infrastructure, trading links, governance system, education system, development of technology, and the "brain drain" has been the obstruction of the transformation process. Therefore, the catching-up process proves to be more difficult than in the case of CEE countries, not only due to the fact that these countries were not home to the armed conflict but because their transition process was not interrupted.

The economic regeneration, influenced by the international financial assistance, started to take place within the implementation of the Dayton Peace Agreement. However, even ten years after the end of the armed conflict and an enormous amount of foreign assets being transferred, the country still lags behind. The estimated level of GDP in BiH in 1999 was only between 35-40% of the level achieved in 1991, with 30% of the GDP being accomplished as a result of the international assistance (Papic, 2002). In 1998, 61% of the population was at the poverty level (Stojanov, 2002). Even though the growth of real GDP is noticeable, it is important to pay attention to the fact that it is

---

[2] The reliability of the statistics from the Western Balkan region remains low and numbers should be interpreted cautiously. Depending on the data available, economic indicators are presented in this paper either in USD or Euro.

calculated based on the 1995 base, a time when BiH's real GDP was extremely low.

Table 1.1: Basic Economic Indicators for BiH, FBiH, RS (1999-2002)

	Real GDP growth (in %) 2003	Nominal GDP per capita (in €) 2002	Inflation (in %) End of 2003	Unemployment rate (in %) 2003
Bosnia and Hercegovina	3.2	1,857.3	0.4	40.6

Source: Altmann F.L. (2004); Sanfley P., Falcetti E., Taci A., Tepic S. (2004)

Government sector expenditures remain very high, with public spending amounting to 56% of the GDP in 2002. Foreign debt is estimated at 52% of the GDP with 50% being owed to the World Bank, 19% to the Paris Club, 5% to the London Club and 4% to the International Monetary Fund (EU Commission, 2003).

BiH is suffering from the grey economy, not only in the area of trade but also concerning employment. Figures of the growth rate of the GDP, trade and the low level of employment in both entities are believed to be considerably underestimated. Smuggling across borders and practices of unregistered employment have been common procedures since the end of the war (Causevic, 2002).

Industrial production remains low and still has not catched up with the pre-war figures. Reasons for the poor competitiveness of the industrial sector are the following:

- overstaffed companies
- outdated technology and marketing methods
- slow and delayed privatization.

The inter-entity trade still stays at a disappointing level. The entities cooperate more with their neighbouring countries (RS with Serbia and Montenegro and FBiH with Croatia) than with each other. Therefore, using trade as an integrative mean strengthening the links between the Entities, which could contribute to the growth of the GDP and improve the functioning of an internal market, is still left aside (Stojanov, 2002).

Due to the pressure and influence of the International Community, especially of the International Monetary Fund and the World Bank, several basic conditions for a functioning economy have been established. In 1998, a new currency was introduced – the convertible mark (KM)[3] which is valid throughout the whole country. In 1997, the BiH Central Bank has started its operations as a currency board with the currency being pegged at a fixed exchange rate first to the Deutsche Mark and since 1999 to the Euro. This has enabled BiH to create a more stable macroeconomic environment with low inflation rates. However, the introduction of the currency board gas raised criticism throughout the country because BiH has lost the advantage of using monetary policy as one of the instruments to influence its economy.[4] Moreover, a fixed exchange rate has hindered better export results by supporting import prices on an artificially cheap level and preventing KM's devaluation (EU Commission, 2003).[5]

Likewise, the International Community has encouraged the start of the privatization process in BiH. After the conclusion of small-scale privatization, which had started in 1999, large-scale privatization is being currently conducted with strategic enterprises being tendered for. In the FBiH, the privatization of large-scale companies with a total value of 8.8 million Euros has been conducted mainly through public share offers (36% of the companies) and tenders (41.2%) that in the latter case proved to be less successful. Out of

---

[3] Before the introduction of the KM, four different currencies were present in BiH: ex-Yugoslav Dinar, Croatian Kuna, Serb Dinar, and Deutsche Mark.

[4] The architects of the Dayton Peace Agreement took this into consideration. However, the lack of any national currency in BiH at that moment combined with the lack of trust in the domestic politicians put these issues aside.

[5] For further information about the currency board in BiH see: Kovacevic. Dragan (2002): The currency board and monetary stability in Bosnia and Hercegovina, Bank for International Settlements, http://www.bis.org/publ/bppdf/bispap17e.pdf.

56 companies prepared for privatization, six were privatized in 2001 and five in 2002 (EU Commission, 2003).

The policy of export expansion remains the priority on the agenda of BiH politicians. However, the key success under the export oriented industrialization lies in the capability of the country to produce what is demanded on the international markets. At present, BiH exports originating from domestic firms are mainly primary commodity and agricultural goods[6] which are often subject to the fluctuations of world market prices. Even though they are destined for the markets of the European Union, their volume has little significance for the economic growth of BiH as well as for the EU markets.

Table 1.2: Main Products in 2000 (in million € and %)

EU Imports	Bosnia share of EU		EU Exports	Bosnia share of EU		Balance
Products	Value	Total by prod.	Products	Value	Total. by prod.	
Agricultural products	93,3	0,12	Agricultural products	193	0,32	99
Energy	0,1	0,0	Energy	25	0,08	25
Machinery	19,6	0,01	Machinery	232	0,08	212
Transport. Material	10,2	0,01	Transport. Material	134	0,09	124
Chemical products	6,4	0,01	Chemical products	93	0,07	87
Textiles and clothing	101,3	0,15	Textiles and clothing	99	0,25	-2

Source: FiFo Ost Database for enterprises, companies, service companies and other economic

Organisations (2003)

Due to the lack of diversified exports and insufficient domestic production capacities, BiH has been suffering from one-sided dependence on

---

[6] Main export products: aluminium alloys, wood roughly trimmed, electric power, hides and skins of bovine animals.

imports composed of consumer goods, raw materials, and machinery. The country's trade deficit has been growing since the end of the war.

Table 1.3: BiH Trade Deficit (in million KM)

	1998	1999	2000	2001	2002
Export	1,168	1,527	2,491	2,494	2,297
Import	6,650	7,579	8,058	8,869	9,319

Source: Central Bank of Bosnia and Hercegovina (2002)

Figure 1.2: BiH Export/Import Destinations (2003)

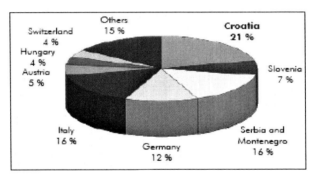

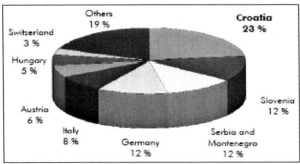

Source: BiH Foreign Investment Promotion Agency (2004)

The reduction of the BiH trade deficit constitutes one of the main challenges for a balanced development of the country. Yet, no major improvements have been visible until present. However, the possibility of an intensified trade within the SEE region (especially with Croatia) might positively stimulate the poor economic situation in BiH.

1.3   Rebuilding the Regional Economic Cooperation in the SEE Area

Main economic arguments encouraging the regional cooperation between transition countries can be assigned to the following categories: increased trade, improvement of political and economic stability, higher investments, and integration in the European Union structures (Uvalic, 2000). The ability to create regional cooperation is considered by the EU bodies as a means to demonstrate that SEE states are capable of sustaining economic relations among each other and with the rest of Europe. Yet, the cooperation between the SEE countries has proven to be rather disappointing in the last decade. During the second half of the 1990s, various initiatives have been undertaken by the International Community in order to assist the SEE countries to revitalize the regional cooperation within the Western Balkan region. However, projects such as the Conference on the Good Neighborliness, Stability, Security and Cooperation in SEE (CSEE), the Royaumont Process as well as the SEE Cooperation Initiative (SECI) did not lead to any substantial results not only due to the fact that they have been imposed from outside but more importantly because most of the programs were not comprehensive enough. The EU early policies directed at the Western Balkans were mainly criticized for the lack of a unified strategy towards the SEE countries. Differential treatments of the individual SEE states and the implementation of more or less favorable policies towards some of the states with respect to others have had a direct impact on their economic performance and transition process (Uvalic, 2000).

The most recent initiative "The Stability Pact" has been introduced in June 1999 by the European Union and the World Bank together with the SEE countries governments and has been considered as one of the most successful

EU initiative to date. One of the aims of the Stability Pact has been the implementation of trade liberalization between the SEE countries.[7] However, instead of a rapid creation of a free trade area, the participating countries decided to sign a Memorandum of Understanding[8] (MoU) on June 21st, 2001 which has established a network of limited bilateral relations. The complicated bilateral approach was influenced by the lack of a political consensus between the SEE states on the formation of a free trade area and economic differences in the level of development of each of the countries. Nevertheless, the MoU set a target date of December 2002 to finish the work on all the agreements. In March 2003, out of 21 potential agreements eight were operational. In case of the agreements, which are still not operational, tariffs on many items have been already lowered or abolished. However, poor coordination of these agreements, which include different products, preferences, and rules of origin for participating parties, might hinder the creation of an effective free trade area in the SEE region (Michalopoulos, 2001).

BiH has been participating in most of the regional initiatives. The country's market is small and due to its political arrangement it is split into several parts with different administrations. The purchasing power remains at a low level and expected growth rates for the coming years are modest. A prospect for increasing market size lies in free trade agreements. Even though the level of BiH exports to the region does not have a significant value at the moment, it is after all the second highest after Croatia. Yet, attention should be paid to the fact that BiH, similarly to the rest of the SEE region, is still suffering from a substantial amount of smuggling especially across some of the "soft" borders for example to Serbia, Republika Srpska, Croatia and Hercegovina.

---

[7] More about the Stability Pact: see the Official website of Special Co-Coordinator of the Stability Pact for South Eastern Europe, http://www.stabilitypact.org .

[8] Signed by Albania, BiH, Bulgaria, Croatia, Macedonia, Romania, Serbia and Montenegro and Moldova.

Table 1.4: Exports to the SEE market (million of $)

	95	96	97	98	99	00	01
Croatia	455	619	732	719	612	537	617
BiH	9	61	31	149	113	75	118
Albania	10	8	10	4	5	3	4
Serbia & Montenegro	0	0	0	1	0	0	1
Macedonia, FYR	57	85	94	87	83	84	96

Source: Antonis (2001)

1.4 The EU Regulations Regarding the Trade between the EU and BiH

At the present time, trade between the EU and Bosnia-Hercegovina is governed by the European Union's autonomous trade preferences, as laid down in the Council Regulation (EC) 2007/2000 of September 18th, 2000. These preferences provide for duty and quota free access of products originating from BiH to the European Union. Only a few exceptions, notably for products such as baby-beef, certain fishery products and wine, apply.

In addition, trade of textile products is governed by a bilateral textile agreement from 2001 which allows free imports from BiH into the EU, subject to a double-checking mechanism guaranteeing surveillance of trade flows between the two partners. At the moment, the EU and BiH do not have any bilateral free trade agreement.

These regulations have been far more generous than the ones offered to the Central and Eastern Europe countries. The CEE states were faced with the various EU import duties and quotas, restrictions between four and five years after the Association Agreements came into force[9]. The reason for the generous trade agreement between the EU and BiH might be due to the low share of EU imports from BiH. In the year 2000, when the regulation entered into force, its share constituted only 0.02% of the total EU imports (Fifo Ost Database, 2003); therefore any possible disruption or even influence of BiH's products on the EU market has been considered as non-existing.

Table 1.5: BiH Exports (2003)

	Exports of goods as % of GDP	Imports of goods as % of GDP	Exports of services as % of GDP	Imports of services as % of GDP	Trade deficit as % of GDP
BiH	21.2	76.9	6.9	4.2	-36.6

Source: Poeschl (2004); Altmann (2004)

Even though the distortion of the immense EU market would not have been possible by BiH products, the duty free access to the European markets probably had a noticeable impact on the export growth and lowering trade deficit in BiH. It possibly not only stimulated the expansion of the local firms but even the inflow of foreign capital wishing to take advantage of the EU regulations. However, in 2002 trade deficit amounted to 7 billion KM with export falling by 8% when compared to 2001 (Central Bank of Bosnia and Hercegovina, 2002). The low volume of exports to the EU markets and the lack of diversification can be explained by lost trading networks, limited awareness of present market trends, insufficient information and visa requirements for BiH citizens (which limits the possibility of business meetings abroad). However, the main obstacle is the EU certification procedure, which represents an effective barrier to increase export volume.

The EU imposes technical standard requirements to all of its trading partners. It has established broad legislation in the area of product standardization and conformity assessment procedure with an aim to provide

---

[9] In the case of Poland, which signed the Association Agreement in 1992 (entered in force in 1994), EU agreed on the full trade liberalisation from 01/01/1998.

proper consumer protection throughout the territory of the European Union member states (Harmonized Standards Legislation). These various EC directives have also created very effective barriers to trade for third parties due to the fact that imposed technical requirements increase the production expenditures and impose new costs arising from obtaining certificates.

Bosnia and Hercegovina has inherited the ex-Yugoslav legislation in the field of certification and standardization (JUS standards). It is operating under 52 mandatory certification schemes based on technological regulations of former Yugoslavia. It has not managed to properly develop relevant bodies responsible for accreditation of the Notified Bodies as well as Notified Bodies capable of granting the EU certificates. There are no official information centers in BiH regarding the technological regulations. Granting of national, mandatory standards, not recognized in the area of the European Union, remains in the competence of the various ministers in the territory of the RS and the FBiH. Not only there has been little development in the transition of the EU certification legislation into national law, but also the directives have been interpreted differently according to the needs of the political parties. Even though the interest of local companies in acquiring the certificates is growing, high costs combined with companies' difficult financial situation have resulted in the limited number of enterprises which actually managed to obtain them.

1.5   Foreign Direct Investments in BiH

FDI are considered as a very good proxy for a country's integration in the international economic networks. Foreigners offer access to global markets, knowledge and management, skills and techniques. They often supply local companies with new technologies and train local executives. More importantly, they provide capital - their own or generated from foreign banks and investors. They play an essential role in the strengthening of the private sector in the host country, emergence of the market economy behavior, and elimination of distortions inherited from the centrally planned systems (United Nations Conference on Trade and Development, 2003).

Not all of the regions where transnational enterprises (TNE) locate their production sites are similarly being developed by the incoming capital. The impact of the FDI on the economic growth of developing regions or countries going through the transition period can differ dramatically. Countries' export roles in the global economy, often imposed by the foreign capital, can have an influence on the upgrading of the economy. However, they are determined by the goals and strategies implemented by the foreign firms. The following table presents the impact of the TNE's strategies.

Table 1.6: TNE's Strategies

	Drawbacks	**Socio-economic structure**	**Economy spillover**
Export processing assemblies	Threat of easy relocation.	Foreign-owned assembly plant combined with home-based work, formal and informal jobs, unskilled and cheap labor, and no unions.	Few links.
Component-supply sub-contracting	TNEs subordinate nat. development to their global profitability.	Local firms and their networks controlled by TNEs.	Allows upgrading, creates backward linkages.
Original equipment manufacturing	TNEs get the biggest gain.	Locally owned contract manufactures, government assistance, and local entrepreneurship.	Allows domestic companies to act on the behalf of TNEs and to become second-tier integrators with less developed regions.

Source: Gereffi (1995)

In most cases, the relations between the TNEs and the domestic governments can influence the development of the given region. A country's growth can be determined by the characteristics of the investment and the host country itself. The nature of the bargaining process between the transnational enterprises and the state officials in the developing regions is influenced by many factors, including the size of the planned investment, the technology requirements, as well as the size of the local market and its potential growth and social mobilization (Moran, 1978).

By the end of the 1980s, Yugoslavia had implemented the most liberal foreign investment rules among the European socially planned economy countries. Therefore, until 1991 it occupied the first place among the CEE countries in terms of number of foreign enterprises and amount of foreign capital invested (Dobosiewicz, 1993). The outbreak of the armed conflict caused the loss of the established networks.

In 1998, BiH passed the Foreign Investment Law, which is fully harmonized throughout the country. It guarantees national treatment of foreign investors, the right to open accounts in any commercial bank or any freely convertible currency, protection against nationalization, expropriation or measures having equivalent effects, repatriation of profits, the right to freely employ foreign nationals (subject to the labor legislation and immigration laws in BIH) and the exemption from payments of custom duties and custom fees for investments.

The two entities have various legislation in the area of tax and company laws. In terms of tax incentives there are also differences. In the FBiH, if the foreign investment exceeds 20% of the company equity (including 100% investment), a company is exempted from the profit taxes for the period of the first five years of its operations (proportionally to foreign stakes in total capital of company). The Republika Srpska provides no tax exemptions (BiH Foreign Investment Promotion Agency, 2002).

BiH has nine free trade zones (eight in the FBiH and one in RS) were additional benefits can be granted to the foreign as well as to the local companies. Goods manufactured or transformed in the zone may also be sold in the local market after payment of duties on imported products (UNCTAD, 2003).

Table 1.7: Basic Market Conditions in RS and FBiH (2002)

	RS	FBiH
Market size (population)	1.4 m.	2.3 m.
Bureaucracy	High	High
Corruption	High	High
Comparative advantages	Wood & metal (bauxite iron ore), building material water power	metal industry, chemical industry, banking

Sources: *Stability Pact Monitoring Instruments; BiH Foreign Investment Promotion Agency (2003)*

The following incentives are being used by the BiH authorities to attract foreign capital:

- economic stability
- preferential export regimes (esp. the case of the EU regulations)
- favorable legislative treatment
- skilled, educated and competitively priced labor force
- privatization (Foreign Investment Promotion Agency, 2004).

Macroeconomic stability is without any doubt an asset. However, the political climate and the complexity of BiH state structure work to BiH's disadvantage. In the case of the preferential export regimes, the EU regulations offer a good opportunity for the EU companies (or any other enterprise possessing the EU certificates) to take advantage of the duty free export to the EU market. Several EU companies have been expressing interest in creating joint ventures with local firms. However, the existing barriers to enter create obstacles that cause many firms to withdraw. Main obstacles hindering the inflow of foreign capital in BiH are:

- existence of unfair trading practices
- administrative barriers to entry (i.e. time needed to register a firm, (in 2001: 120 days))

- no harmonized laws concerning ownership and transfer of ownership of all types of real estate
- lack of harmonization of tax laws
- ineffectiveness of the juridical system in resolving business disputes
- corruption
- poorly developed transportation infrastructure
- not sufficient measures to support entrepreneurship.[10]

In terms of labor, labor costs remain to be competitive not only in comparison with the EU countries but also within the CEE states. The population is educated and skilled. However, the problem remains in the area of how to implement their knowledge into practice, especially in the manufacturing sector. The theoretical background (especially in the technical field), which is being acquired at schools, is not matched by practical preparation. The employees are often not familiar with current equipment and machines used by foreign companies and have difficulties in their maintenance. Therefore, foreigners are often faced with the need of "importing" their own specialists (Hofert, 2003).

Moreover, due to the country's difficult financial situation and a high unemployment rate, BiH is confronted with the outflow of educated population (brain drain), mostly to Western Europe countries and the USA. This is one of the most severe consequences of the war. Most of the refugees is highly qualified, as well as the school-age population. However, after completing their university education abroad, they will probably never return. The process of exodus started to take place already during the war but escalated greatly after the end of the armed conflict. From 1996-98 the total number of emigrants from BiH was estimated at 42 thousand people. The United Nations Development Program research from 2000 has shown that 62% of the country's youth would like to leave BiH (Papic, 2002).

---

[10] For further information on administrative barriers to enter see: Bosnia and Hercegovina (2001). Commercial Legal Framework and Administrative Barriers to Investment, Foreign Investment Advisory Centre (World Bank Group), http://www.fias.net

The favorable legislation being considered as an asset can be questioned as well. Even though the BiH government passed all the necessary laws to attract foreign capital, the slow implementation phase and differences between the Entities in this matter still discourage the inflow of FDI. The works of the relevant State and Entity institutions still require major improvement

As for the privatization being considered an asset, major doubt expressed concerning the conduct of the process itself, its speed, lack of transparency and corruption. There has been more and more open request for the revision of the privatization which has gained acceptance neither from the public nor in some cases from the International Community.[11] If the process will not be accelerated and no steps will be undertaken to eliminate irregularities, it is highly doubtful that foreign investors who seek a safe legal framework, will turn their attention to BiH (BiH Ministry of Foreign Trade and Economic Relations, 2002).

All of these issues have been reflected in the value of foreign direct investments attracted by BiH. In the period from 1995 to 2002, they amounted for only 805 million KM. However, there has been an increase of the inflow in 2004 compared to 2002. Nevertheless, its value still remains very low when compared to Croatia, which managed to attract only till 2001 1.85 billion Euro (UNDP, 2003).

---

[11] Privatisation process in Canton 1 can be given as en example.

Figure 1.3: FDI in BiH 1994-2004 (in thousand €)

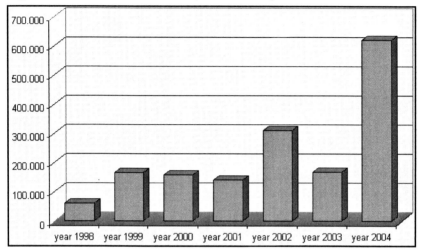

Source: BiH Foreign Investment Promotion Agency (2004)

As discussed above, BiH is not experiencing a high volume of FDI inflow. Countries expressing interest in locating their investments in BiH are mainly the ex-Yugoslav republics (Croatia, Slovenia, Serbia and Montenegro), Arabic countries (Kuwait) and a few EU member states. There is practically no interest from the CEE states. There are clear indicators showing that the placement of the investments is connected with the ethnical division of the country (i.e. Arabic countries invest only in FBiH inhabited by the Muslim population) which might not always correspond to the best resource allocation.

BiH is currently involved in the re-creation of lost investment links, especially within the SEE region and the European Community with varying degree of success. However, the value of investments remains modest.

Table 1.8: Biggest Country-Investors in BiH (1994-2004)

	(million Euro)
Croatia	264,9
Austria	220,3
Slovenia	150,9
Germany	124,0
Holland Antilles	119,3
Kuwait	101,0
Serbia and Montenegro	85,4
The Netherlands	58,9
Italy	50,6

Source: *BiH Foreign Investment Promotion Agency (2004)*

The composition of the FDI inflow to BiH has been quite disappointing until present. In most of the cases they have been attracted by privatization related issues and not by market-seeking nature. They have been concentrated in the manufacturing and banking services. Investments in these sectors contribute to the efficiency of resource allocation, but not too much to sustainable growth. Additionally, there is a small share of export orientated and Greenfield investments. The reasons behind the present FDI structure can be found in the risky investment environment (Zakharov & Kušić, 2003).

Table 1.9: FDI in BiH by Sectors (1994-2004)

Production	59,40%
Banking	14,50%
Trade	6,4 %
Services	4,20%
Transport	4,1 %
Tourism	2,30%
Others	9,1 %

Source: *BiH Foreign Investment Promotion Agency (2004)*

The current inflow of FDI still remains at an insufficient level for the successful economic development of BiH and its structure does not create many spillover effects. The presence of foreign capital contributes mainly to the creation or sustaining work force participation. Obstacles such as administrative barriers to entry and problems connected with the privatization of state owned companies discourage potential investors and make them choose other transition countries (i.e. Croatia) that provide similar incentives and that are better prepared in terms of institutional capacity, government effectiveness, and control of corruption (see the graphs below).

Figure 1.4: Governance Indicators in Croatia (2004)

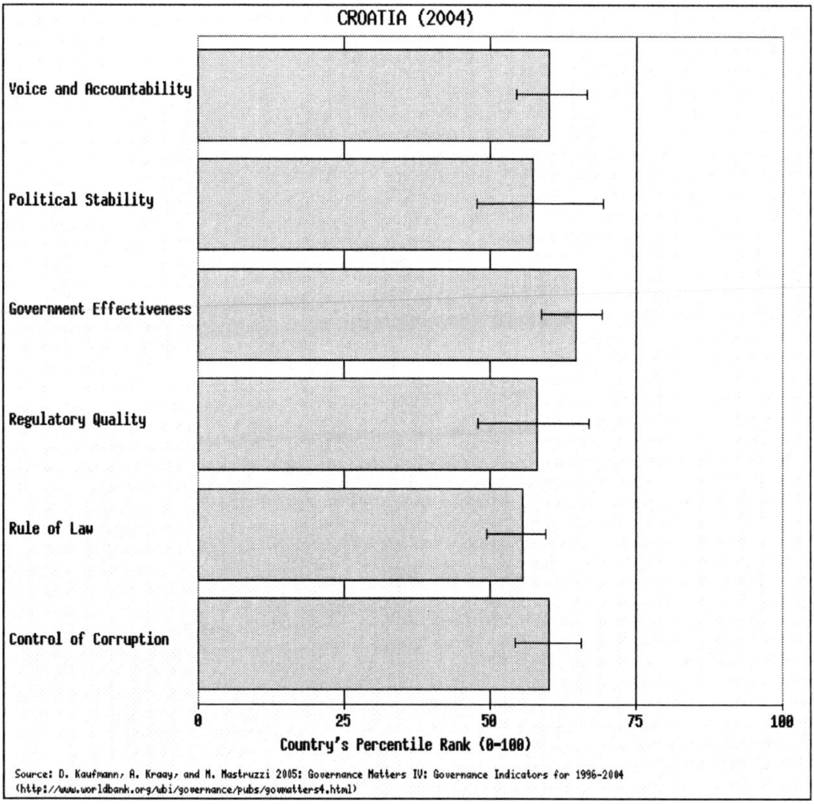

Source: D. Kaufmann, A. Kraay, and M. Mastruzzi 2005: Governance Matters IV: Governance Indicators for 1996-2004 (http://www.worldbank.org/wbi/governance/pubs/gowmatters4.html)

Figure 1.5: Governance Indicators in BiH (2004)

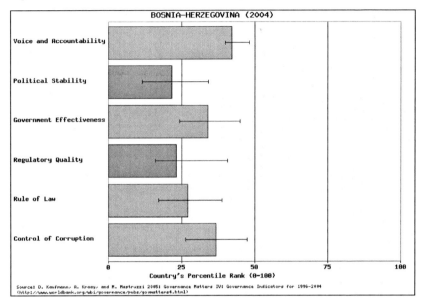

BiH political insecurity, lack of accountability among politicians, fragmentation of the markets and hesitant market reforms has kept away foreign investors (United Nations Conference on Trade and Development, 2003).

Among the investing countries, the share of the EU companies has increased over the last few years in the SEE countries, including BiH. However, it still remains much lower than in the CEE states. This situation can be blamed not only on the above-mentioned obstacles but also on the BiH's weak world image. It is not without any reason that the country is being perceived as a corrupted post war area with a lack of political stability. Furthermore, there is not enough support for inflow of foreign capital in the society which is only looking at the negative side of FDI (the possible lay offs once the companies are privatized and crowding out of the domestic firms) (The BiH Ministry of Foreign Trade and Economic Relations, 2003).

However, the major opportunity for attracting more foreign investments is the prospectus integration with the EU structures. The possibility of admission to the EU, once the conditions for the membership have been fulfilled, might, as in the case of CEE countries, encourage the higher inflow of foreign capital and thus improve the overall BiH economic development.

1.6   Concluding Remarks

The creation of conditions for the success of Bosnia and Hercegovina as a functioning state, presents a major task for the International Community, including the European Union as well as the BiH government authorities. Yet, ten years after the end of the armed conflict, the country still has not made a significant economic progress, as it has been seen in the case of Croatia. The economic backwardness has been caused, without any doubt, by the military actions. However, the limited progress achieved until present indicates that the complicated political structure which contributes to the limited cooperation between the governmental bodies restrains quick economic restructuring. Naturally, it cannot be claimed that the entities' existence constitutes BiH's major drawback, yet the lack of an alliance between them does. If not for the ever-existing competition among them, the central government weak powers would not constitute a hindrance. However, in the present situation where the political arena is used mainly for the "blame the other" speeches, does create a disadvantage to the BiH economic development. The difficulties in reaching a decision, the duplication of governmental institutions and a very expensive administration system which BiH cannot afford has resulted in a budget deficit and lack of state efficiency. Furthermore, deficit of any political accountability has created enormous barriers for an effective implementation of the needed reforms.

Successful transition from the command economy system and reconstruction of the country should have happened at much faster pace, especially after taking in consideration the IC's financial assistance transferred to BiH after 1995. The extremely preferential trade regime, not offered to the CEE states during their transition process, should have resulted in the reduction of the trade deficit, yet it did not. On the contrary, the import dependence has been growing.

BiH did not take the advantage of being a "late comer" to the world markets. Distracted by the political disputes, mainly caused by the entities' hostility towards each other, it has managed to restrain the revitalization of the lost trading links, thus gave an opportunity to its neighboring countries or the CEE states to step in. The inflow of the foreign capital has not been sufficient enough to provide technology transfers and to create positive spillover effects. Moreover, the present BiH export role in the world markets places the country almost at the bottom of the Gereffi's scale. Exports of the primary commodities, often victim to the fluctuations of the world prices put BiH in a disadvantaged position. Activities of foreign investors present in the country (manufacturing and banking sector) contribute to the efficiency of resource allocation, but not too much to sustainable growth. Hope remains in upcoming eastern enlargement of the EU, when the EU investors might turn their attention to BiH.

The chance for BiH to catch up still exists. However, the gap between is - and could be with time - getting more impassable. Whether the gap will disappear depends on the willingness of the government authorities at the state, entities, and cantonal level to cooperate with each other.

Bibliography

ALTMANN F.-L. (2004): Regional Economic Problems and Prospects, In: Batt Judy (ed.), The Western Balkans: Moving on, Chaillot Paper, No 70, Institute for Security Studies, Paris.

ANNUAL REPORT (2002): The Central Bank of Bosnia and Hercegovina, p. 65, http://www.cbbh.gov.ba.

ANTONIS, A., KOSMA, T., AND MCHUGH, J. (2003): Trade Liberalization Strategies: What could South Eastern Europe Learn from CEFTA and BFTA, European Trade Study Group (ETSG), Paper presented during the ETSG Conference, 11-13.09.2003, Madrid, The ETSG website, http://www.etsg.org/ETSG2002/papers/adam.pdf.

BIH (2003): Enhancing Business Climate to Attract Domestic and Foreign Investments Office of BiH Co-ordinator for Poverty Reduction Strategy Paper, The BiH Ministry of Foreign Trade and Economic Relations.

BOSNIA AND HERCEGOVINA COUNTRY PROFILE (2002): United Nations Conference on Trade and Development, http://www.unctad.org.

CAUSEVIC, F. (2002): Employment and Privatization, in: Papic, Zarko (Eds): International Support Policies to South-East European Countries, Lessons (Not) Learned in BiH. Mueller, Sarajevo, pp. 92-93.

COMMISSION OF THE EUROPEAN COMMUNITIES (2003): Bosnia and Hercegovina Stabilization and Association Report 2003, Commission Staff Working Paper, Brussels, p.19.

DOBOSIEWICZ, Z. (1993): Foreign Investments in Eastern Europe. Routledge, London, p.75.

FIFO Ost Database for Enterprises, Companies, Service Companies and other Economic Organization. http://www.fifoost.org.

FOREIGN INVESTMENT PROMOTION AGENCY OF BIH (2002): Investors Guide for Bosnia and Hercegovina, BiH Foreign Investment Promotion Agency, Sarajevo.

FOREIGN TRADE CHAMBER OF BOSNIA AND HERCEGOVINA (2003): accessed on 09/09/2003, http://www.fias.net.

FOREIGN INVESTMENT ADVISORY CENTRE (WORLD BANK GROUP) (2001): Bosnia and Hercegovina, Commercial Legal Framework and Administrative Barriers to Investment, http://www.fias.net.

GEREFFI, G. (1995) Global Production Systems & the 3rd World Development, In: Stallings, Barbara. (Eds.): Global Change, Regional Response, Cambridge, Cambridge University Press, pp.100-142.

HOFERT, A. (2003): Vorschlag Ausbildung in der Region Banja Luka: Republik Srpska.

KEANE, R. (2002): Reconstituting Sovereignty. Post-Dayton Uncovered, Hampshire, Ashgate Publishing, 2002, p. 73.

KOVACEVIC, D. (2003): The Currency Board and Monetary Stability in Bosnia and Hercegovina, http://www.bis.org/publ/bppdf/bispap17e.pdf.

MICHALOPOULOS, C. (2001): The Western Balkans in World Trade, The World Bank, Washington, p.10.

MORAN, T. (1978): Multinational Cooperations and Dependency: A Dialogue for Dependentistas and Non- Dependentistas. International Organization, No.1, pp.79-100.

PAJIC, Z. (1999): A Critical Appraisal of the Human Rights Provisions of the Dayton Constitution of Bosnia & Hercegovina, in: Wolfgang Benedek (Eds.): Human Rights in Bosnia and Hercegovina after Dayton: From Theory to Practice, Hague: Kluwer Law International.

PAPIC, Z. (2002): The General Situation in BiH and International Support Policies, in: Papic, Z. (eds). International Support Policies to South-East European Countries, Lessons (Not) Learned in BiH, Mueller: Sarajevo, pp.18-19.

POESCHL, J. (2004): Trade-Offs & Ways Out, In: Solioz, Christophe/Vogel, Tobias K. (Eds.). Dayton and Beyond: perspectives on the Future of Bosnia & Hercegovina, Nomos Verlaggesellschaft, pp. 134

SANFLEY, P. AND FALCETTI, E., TACI, A., TEPIC, S. (2004): Spotlight on South-Eastern Europe, An Overview of Private Sector Activity and Investment, European Bank for Reconstruction and Development, p.6.

STOJANOV, D. (2002): BiH since 1995: Transition and Reconstruction of the Economy, in: Papic, Z. (Eds). International Support Policies to South-East European Countries, Lessons (Not) Learned in BiH, Mueller: Sarajevo, p.64-70.

THE INTERNATIONAL BANK FOR RECONSTRUCTION AND DEVELOPMENT / THE WORLD BANK (2004): Building Market Institution in South Eastern Europe, Comparative Prospects for Investment and Private Sector Development, pp.x-xxi.

The Official website of the German Foreign Affairs Ministry (2002): Bosnia and Hercegovina, Economic Policy, http://www.auswaertiges-amt.de.

The Official website of the Bosnia and Hercegovina Foreign Investment Promotion Agency, http://www.fipa.go.ba.

The Official website of the Organization for Security & Cooperation in Europe, Mission to Bosnia and Hercegovina, http://www.oscebih.org.

The Official website of the UN Development Programme, http://www.undp.org

The Official website of Special Co-Coordinator of the Stability Pact for South Eastern Europe, http://www.stabilitypact.org.

UVALIC, M. (2000): Regional Cooperation and Economic Integration in South-Eastern Europe, Economic and Social Research Council, p.10, http://www.one-europe.ac.uk/events/2000/conference/Uvalicpaper.pdf

WORLD INVESTMENT DIRECTORY (2003): Central and Eastern Europe, 2003 Volume III, United Nations, p.10, United Nations Conference on Trade and Development, http://www.unctad.org.

ZAKHAROV, V., AND KUŠIĆ, S. (2003): The Role of FDI in EU Accession Process: The Case of Western Balkans. European Trade Study Group (ETSG), Paper presented at the ETSG Conference, 11-13.09.2003, Madrid, p. 3, The ETSG website, http://www.etsg.org/ETSG2002/papers/adam.pdf.

Chapter 2

Daniel Göler:

Integration and Peripherisation Processes in the Western Balkans – Problems of Regional Development in Albania

2.1 Growing Disparities and the European Perspective – a brief Outline of the Problem

The various integration and peripherisation processes along the EU-border are one of the major problems concerning future spatial development in East and Southeast Europe. With hardly any reasonable doubt one can say that the future of the countries on the Western Balkans[12] lies in their further approach to or in joining the common European economic union. According to Altmann (2003a, p.175) the integration is an "option without alternatives". No matter whether it is considered a medium or long-term perspective, whether the integration will be gradually realized or en bloc, what the conditions are that will have to be fulfilled by new members, or even how the EU will have to adapt the current structural funds to the new situation – concrete statements are still within the bounds of speculation.

Against such a background, the region's fragmentation into small units, the barely calculable potential for conflicts, the enormous disparities in development and the economic dependencies on the Western Balkans are a challenge both from a regional point of view and as a practical task. For the

---

[12] In EU-jargon the term "Western Balkans" is commonly used for Albania as well as the successor states of former Yugoslavia, i.e. Bosnia-Hercegovina, Croatia, Macedonia and (the two now discrete states) Serbia and Montenegro (including Kosovo) (Altmann 2003a, p.175)

region the European perspective appears to be a solution and a problem at the same time (Meurs, 2003, p.35). The following paper is an attempt to contribute to the central topic "The Western Balkans on their Way to the EU" by presenting a number of selected aspects illustrated at the concrete example of Albania's regional development. The crucial points are going to be analyzed with an economic-geographical approach. The spatial categorization and evaluation will be followed by a discussion of potential consequences. The main focus will be set on the very contradictory regional development and the increasing disparities in Albania. At present, both the integration and peripherisation processes become apparent, but they seem to be a typical feature of all countries on the Western Balkans. It leads to the thesis that with ongoing spatial polarization the emerging disparities – apart from the already existing regional ones within the country - could become an obstacle to a future EU-membership.

2.2   Transformation and Fragmentation Processes in the Former Eastern Bloc

The transition processes in former socialist countries lead to a profound and, at the same time, highly heterogeneous socio-economic development. Seen from a spatial-geographical point of view, these countries, even those with a rather similar starting point, do not show a common development. The thesis of convergence, put forward at the beginning of the 1990s has turned out to be inaccurate during following years (Burdack/Rudolph, 2001). At least during the 1990s there were many different ways and levels of development to be observed: On a national level, the Central European and the Baltic countries were quickly integrated into the EU whereas the integration of other nations especially in Southeast Europe is delayed. On a sub-national level, it is mainly the difference between bigger agglomerations and rural areas that appears to be a regular pattern of transition. Usually, transformation processes were a lot more dynamic in the national centers than in rural or peripheral regions with the latter ones being left behind in their economic development (Stadelbauer, 2000, p.62). This is to some extent an indication of persistence of core-periphery-relations form the socialist period.

Fuelled by the ongoing integration and peripherisation, enormous disparities have developed – and that is not only true from a global or European perspective, but also between and often within countries in transition itself. The third report on cohesion of the EU states, for example, that the ratio between GDP-shares of the wealthiest 20% of regional population and the least wealthy 20% was rapidly increasing between 1995 and 2002 (in the Czech Republic from 1.8 up to 2.1, in Poland from 1.6 to 1.9 and in Hungary from 2.0 to 2.6; Commission of the European Communities, 2005, p.20). Even at the beginning of the third millennium such diverging ways of development continue to exist. And that is particularly the case in Southeast Europe or rather on the Western Balkans (see Petrakos, Totev, 2001, p.3f.) where disparities on a smaller scale, e.g. in Albania, have already reached an enormous extent.

2.3   Albania in its Western Balkan Context

Even considering the difficult history and the various problems the Western Balkan countries have been facing especially during the 1990s Albania remains a special case. One aspect that separates Albania from others is the very special way of endogenous economic development pursued by the former dictator Hoxha (Russ, 1979) which gradually separated the country not only from Western Countries but also from the Eastern bloc. The nearly complete isolation in the last years of socialism has been the cause of many difficulties the small country had to face at the beginning of its transition process. The industrial production chains, e.g. in branches like metallurgy or mechanical engineering, laboriously built up over decades, suddenly turned out, like many other industries to be internationally not competitive. Industrial production declined to vanishing point. While the agricultural sector was still a kind of constant factor during the transition process with a relative growth in the number of jobs (Doka, 2001, p.339), the now redundant workforce poured into the extremely underdeveloped tertiary sector. Here, especially the consumer orientated sector (i.e. retail trade, bars, cafes and restaurants etc.), showed quite a dynamic development (Becker, Göler, 2000), even though most of the new private businesses were rather small. This first and cautious period of consolidation in the mid 1990s came to an abrupt end by the crash of dubious investment companies. Since anticipated profits were high, countless Albanians invested all their savings in dubious pyramid schemes and lost everything (Korovilas, 1999). In its wake, the country went through civil-war-like conditions between March and June 1997 (Mema, Dika, 2005, p.196). The material damage caused by sheer destructive urge was severe by any means, but from today's point of view the loss of confidence of potential foreign investors was by far more serious. Although Albania was not affected directly by the Kosovo War a few years later, its image suffered once more. Until the present day, the economic crisis is seen as just another evidence of the permanent instability of the entire region. The "systemic weaknesses" (Dobrinsky, 2001, p.69ff.) result from fragile economic structures as well as weak institutional infrastructures. Both are signs of a highly vulnerable system which became particularly evident in Albania during the 1990s. The many interruptions to the transition process, apart from the low starting point, are the reason for the country's slow progress. A comparison of statistical socio-economic figures of the five countries on the Western Balkans shows that Albania is far behind Croatia, but rather on the level of Bosnia-Hercegovina, which suffered war damage.

Table 2.1: The Countries of the Western Balkans – Statistically Compared

Indicator*	AL	BiH	CS	HR	MK
Population in million (2004)	3,2	4,2	10,5	4,4	2,1
Area in sqm	28.748	51.197	102.173	56.542	25.713
GDP in million USD (2002)	4.835	5.599	15.681	22.436	3.791
GDP real/head, in USD	1.278	1.675	1.830	5.440	2.429
Annual GDP growth in % (2002)	4,7	3,9	4,0	5,2	0,7
GDP share of primary sector (2003)**	24,7	14,9	k.A.	8,4	12,2

... of secondary sector **	19,2	32,1	k.A.	30,1	30,4
... of tertiary sector**	56,1	53,0	k.A.	61,5	57,3
Imports (in mio. USD 2003)	1.835	3.992	5.844	14.136	2.241
Exports (in mio.USD 2003)	446	1.113	1.704	6.162	1.351
Balance of trade (in mio. USD 2003)	-1.389	-2.879	-4.140	-7.975	-890
FDI 2004 (million USD)***	350	420	950	1100	150
Share of internet users (per 1,000 inhabitants, 2003)	10	26	79	232	48
Cars (per 1000 inhabitants, 2003)	43	31	136	280	152
% of population below nat. poverty line (2002)	25,4	20,0	10,0	10,0	22,7
Spending power/head 2005 (preisbereinigt in €)*****	1482	3306	3573	6313	3163
HDI 2002****	0,781	0,781	k.A.	0,830	0,793
Reform indicator 2004***	2,8	2,5	2,5	3,4	3,0

(AL: Albania, BiH: Bosnia and Hercegovina, CS: Serbia and Montenegro including Kosovo, HR: Croatia, MK: Macedonia)

---

*   *Source, if not indicated differently: Statistisches Bundesamt der BRD (Statistics Office of the Fed. Rep. of Germany), www.destatis.de/ausl_prog/suche_ausland.htm (4.4.2005)*

**   *Source: World Bank, http://web.worldbank.org (3.6.2005)*

***   *Source: EBRD (European Bank for Reconstruction and Development; http://www.ebrd.com/pubs/ar/deutsch/04/6390.pdf (3.6.2005); criteria for the indicator are 9 reform indicators, maximum at 4,33.*

****   *Source: UN, http://hdr.undp.org/statistics/data/pdf/hdr04_table_1.pdf (3.6.20005)*

***** *Source: GfK group (company for consume research), press report from 3.5.2005 ("Oft liegen arm und reich beieinander"); IMOE-Osteuropa-aktuell Newsletter 5/2005, 18.5.2005, published by the Informationsagentur Mittel- und Osteuropa (Information agency for Central and East Europe).*

A constant outlet for all the problems of transformation and for the difficult economic situation inside the country has been (and it is as ever) the temporary or permanent emigration (King, 2004). Although the storming of the embassies by refugees in 1990 was spectacular, it was a quantitatively unimportant and spontaneous aspect of emigration. Nevertheless it was a signal for the later mass-exodus. According to reliably estimations, at least 750,000 Albanians left their country during the 1990s, mainly to Italy and Greece. Financial support by these Albanian expatriates is still an important contribution to the Albanian national economy (Göler, 2005a). The fact that almost 50% of the population left their home temporarily or at least forever during the transition period (between the national censuses of 1989 and 2001, Berxholi et al., 2003, p.69) is another evidence for the country's mobilization in post-socialist era.

The internal migration is quite a useful indicator of structural disparities in Albania. While the capital and its surrounding area – the Tirana-Durres conurbation is the main focus of migrants and also investments – currently seems to develop highly dynamical, the regions in the North, East and South of Albania (the migrants' origins) show significant tendencies of marginalisation, spatially exemplified, e.g., in deserted settlements (see chapter 2.4.2). At the same time the migrants support the socio-economic changes indirectly because the exodus of young and middle-aged people is always connected with substantial brain-drain and loss of human capital, since the migrants are not from underprivileged classes only (Göler, 2005b).

The population shifts from the periphery to the centre contribute to the current situation of contrary developments in Albania. While the centre is gradually integrated both globally and in Europe, the periphery is faced with growing exclusion and marginalization. In the following paragraphs these two aspects shall be put in a more concrete form by giving empirical results.

Figure 2.1: Albania – an Overview

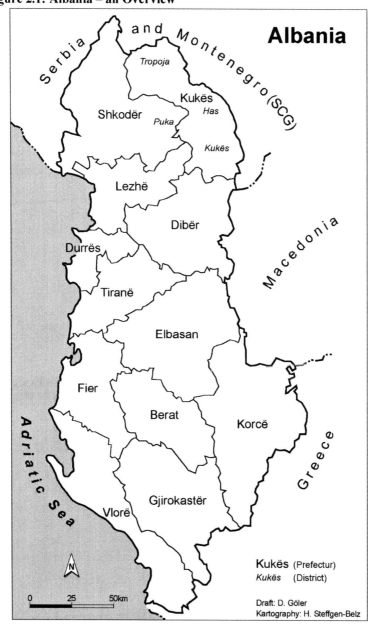

2.4   Regional Aspects of Integration and Peripherisation in Albania

After 1990, Albania's first steps towards integration into the global economic system were more or less a one-way street. The country has been "faced with a collapse of its industrial base" (Petrakos, Totev, 2001, p.11). At the same time demand for consumer goods exploded. Like in other countries in transition, the Albanian market has been flooded with foreign products. This situation has changed only slightly: In 2003, the value of all imports was more than four times the value of exports (Figure 2.1). At the beginning, integration was almost limited to imports of necessary consumer goods. But over the last years, outsourced industries from abroad (job processing industries) pushed into Albania in great numbers. This is a rather new phenomenon and in some extent a first sign of a 'real' economic integration of Albania as a business location into international production systems.

2.4.1   *The Integration of Central Albania – the Example of Job Processing Industries[13]*

Since the mid 1990s and in particular after the unrest of 1996/1997, a number of new manufacturing businesses have been put up in Albania, especially in Greater Tirana. The companies, many of which due to legal requirements are organised as joint ventures with mostly Greek, Italian or Turkish majority shareholders, have chosen Albania for several reasons.

Albania's capital is relatively easy to reach from other EU-countries. First, the main port in Durres and Tirana is connected by a modern expressway

---

[13] The explanations on the phenomenon of job processing industries, also known as low wages industries, in Albania are a result of empirical studies on industrial locations carried out in the Tirana agglomeration under authors' participation in May 2000 (see Becker et al. 2002, in particular p. 6f.)

which makes it easy to reach Tirana by lorries via ferry-boat from Italy; the same can be stated concerning the connection to Greece by road. Second, the level of wages is still very low, and there is a huge workforce (unemployment is still high). And third, there are old factory sheds on brownfield sites – the locations of former combines from communist times–, the conversion of which requires only minimal expenditures. These factors and locational advantages are mainly used for labor intensive productions like in the former textile combine "Josef Stalin", in the tractor factory "Enver Hoxha" or in the former electrotechnical combine "Dinamo". The textile industry (clothes, leather, shoes) is one of the most common users of these locations. Usually, prefabricated parts and all the necessary material is delivered, which are then processed into semi-finished products or increasingly more finished products ready for dispatch. The products are not intended for the Albanian, but for the EU-market. Apart from cheap textiles of lower quality, there are also some well-known brands. Nevertheless, the origin is rather the more trustworthy "Made in Germany", "Made in Italy" or "Made in Greece" than "Made in Albania".

Job processing is encouraged by customs: Since the products do not reach the Albanian market (at least not directly), duties are reduced to only 50% and export (i.e. the return) is duty free. The companies are structured and legally organized in many different ways; there are joint ventures, as mentioned above, as well as companies with 100% Albanian shareholders. What they all have in common is the relation to a single foreign partner or client. The processing level varies from product to product. Top clothes are usually fully completed, whereas in the case of a shoe manufacturer only the upper leathers are sewed in Albania while the more complicated fitting of the soles is done in Italy.

An important aspect is that nearly all companies have no significant purchase or sales connections in Albania itself. Industry-related services are just rarely made use of; usually it is limited to security services. Further spin off effects, a possible basis for a more sustainable economic integration, are not to be expected. Only taxation and particularly the job market act as main links to the Albanian national economy. Various risks like interdependencies or a latent proneness to being affected by negative economic trends or crisis, raise doubts whether job processing has a real potential for future developments.

For a long time, the outsourcing phenomenon has been considered a typical feature of industrialisation in developing countries (Schamp, 2000, p.163ff.), but as seen above, the conditions of socio-economic transition processes make it also a feature of the new economic start in many former Eastern-bloc countries. Job-processing is therefore a new element in the international division of industrial production. Looking at spatial patterns, Schamp (2000, p.165) particularly indicates the local character of these industries, thus attributing a highly spatial polarization to these processes (as well as other business activities) also noticeable in Albania. The given example is by far not the only evidence of industrial embeddedness based on integration of the central Albanian agglomeration.

Typically enough, it was left to the global player Coca-Cola in 1994 to set an example by investing in Albania's first major greenfield site during the early period of transition. It is also typical that the investment was not so much lead by anticipated profits – production still has to struggle with common difficulties like poor infrastructure or security problems – but by being present on the Albanian market. Further evidence for the aspect of integration is given by the efforts of foreign companies to exploit the country's oil and gas resources even though they are very limited.[14]

In mentioning the ongoing integration of the Tirana-Durres agglomeration or Central Albania in the manufacturing sector one must not forget the building and construction industry. There an endogenous development could be easily diagnosed. Even though many parts (especially tiles, sanitation etc.) are imported, the basic materials (sand, gravel, chalk, cement etc.) are mostly from Albania. At the moment, enormous investments

---

[14] This does not refer so much to a return to oil drilling in the Fier region of Central Albania (which started during the early 20th century), than to the off-shore projects in the Karavastase lagoon near Vlora to obtain gas which have been under much criticism even in Albania from an environmental point of view.

are under way – partly by Albanians living abroad, partly from inside the country – that can be seen in Tirana (Becker, Friemer, Göler, 2005). What adds to all this is the city's unquestionable position of a primate city that derives from its status as the dominant centre of power, culture and education in Albania. And after all, Tirana is the focus of internal migration (Table 2.2), a phenomenon that raises the aspect of the periphery as a region which economically marginalized and losing more and more of its population (Göler, 2005).

2.4.2 The Peripherisation of the Hinterland – Structural Characteristics and the Effects of Migration to the Cities

Outside the region of Lower and Central Albania, the situation is completely different. The marginalisation of the Albanian hinterland is most striking with an analysis of demographic processes and settlement structures of the post-socialist period. Doing so, the system of strictly regulated mobility during communist times has to be kept in mind. In this respect, the ban on almost any cross-border-migration is well-known. But also the internal migration was strictly controlled: For example the population was directed to partly newly built towns during the period of rebuilding the economy in the 1970s. Due to a latent food crisis, this policy was replaced from the late 1970s on by directed migration into rural and also peripheral areas with agriculture (Göler, 2005a, p.119f). A special type of settlement, agricultural towns, came into existence. Concerning the effects of Albania's policy, Lawson and Saltmarshe (2000, p.143) state that "the population in the Albanian Highlands was unsustainably large" at the end of the socialist period. During the disintegration of socialist structures, big farms were broken up completely (as reported in detail by Kaser (2002, p.174ff.) on an example from the south Albanian Kurvelesh) taking away the region's source of income. As a result of privatization, the agricultural sector is now divided into a large number of small units that can only exist on a subsistence level. Therefore it seems to be only a logic consequence that the overpopulation in areas like Northern Albania has led to a massive drop in population figures. Leaving their homes, usually with Tirana as the main destination, has surely been the easiest way to solve the problem of job loss (the loss of the economic basis), even though migration has been not automatically connected with a better quality of life due to high unemployment and a difficult housing market at the destination (Friemer, 2004).[15]

Table 2.2: Internal Migration in Albania during Transition Period:

(Population number and internal migration in Albania 1989-2001 by prefecture)

Area		Population			Internal Migration			
Prefecture	Macro-region	1989	2001	Change	Immi-grants	Emi-grants	Balance	Efficiency[*]
Durres	Centre/Coast	218530	245179	26649	44859	7288	37571	72
Elbansan	Centre/Coast	357497	362736	5239	6767	26645	-19878	-59
Fier	Centre/Coast	379342	382544	3202	21343	16536	4807	12
Lezha	Centre/Coast	165254	159182	-6072	10697	11945	-1248	-5
Tirana	Centre/Coast	449228	597899	148671	136576	6351	130225	91
Dibra	North-East	226324	189854	-36470	1682	49084	-47402	-93
Kukes	North-East	146081	111393	-34688	1039	43178	-42139	-95
Shkodra	North-East	285258	256473	-28785	3815	19408	-15593	-67
Berat	South-East	222901	193020	-29881	4260	25676	-21416	-71
Gjirokastera	South-East	155998	112831	-43167	2686	17098	-14412	-72
Korca	South-East	311448	265182	-46266	5874	23469	-17595	-59
Vlora	South-East	264556	192982	-71574	13137	6057	7080	36

* *Migration Efficiency Index: Migration balance divided through the total of migration*

Source: INSTAT (2004): Migration in Albania, p.12/14; own calculation

As Table 2.2 shows, there was a massive decrease in population both in North and in South Albania between the censuses of 1989 and 2001. From a quantitative point of view, the depopulation in South Albania is strongest

---

[15] Many migrants settled or still settle in informal residential areas. Most of them live in the still growing suburban fringe surrounding Tirana (Heller, Doka, Berxholi, 2004). To some extent, real marginal settlements emerged, e.g. in former industrial areas (Becker et al., 2005).

(Delvina district in Saranda prefecture: minus 54.8%). There are many different reasons why people leave the South of the country to go abroad, mainly to Greece.[16] Particularly for the Greek minority in South Albania it is relatively easy to enter the country in order to find legal work; so migration is primarily caused by pull factors in its target area.

Table 2.3: Selection of North Albanian Districts – Statistically Compared

	Puka	Dibra	Kukes	Has	Tropo-ja	Albania
Population (2001)	34.386	85.699	63.786	19.660	27.947	3.069.275
Population change 1989 -2001 (%)	-29,8	-13,8	-19,7	-10,2	-37,6	-3,6
Share of urban population (2001)	17,5	16,4	26,1	16,4	26,8	42,2
Population density (2001)	32,5	88,3	68,4	48,9	25,9	108,2
Rate of unemploy-ment (2001)	26,7	27,1	33,8	29,3	21,2	22,7
Dependency ratio (2001)	67,1	68,3	73,4	80,8	66,0	58,3
People employed in agricultural sector (%)	68,9	60,4	54,5	62,8	57,8	50,5

Source: INSTAT (2002), INSTAT (2004)

In North Albania it is mainly the internal migration destined to Tirana that led to a decrease in population despite a natural increase (due to a still high birth rate). The decrease ranges between 10% (Has district, in Kukes prefecture), nearly 30% in the Puka district (Shkodra prefecture) and up to 38% in the Tropoja district (part of Kukes prefecture; Table 2.3). Contrary to South

---

[16] Additional factors may be spatial proximity, knowledge of the language as well as cultural familiarity. Hathiprokopiou (2005, p. 172) indicates a revival of old mobility patterns, with the migration network between Thessaloniki (Greece) and Korça (South Albania) as an example.

Albania, outmigration from the Northern parts of the country has its roots obviously more in poverty, a fact also shown by ratios of socio-economic indicators far below the Albanian average: The official rate of unemployment in Kukes is as high as 34%. Between 2/3 (Tropoja) and 4/5 (Has) of the total population are, as indicated by the dependency ratio, economically dependent on the income of others. Employment in the agricultural sector is well above 50%, in the Puka district it is at 70%. The share of urban population in four out of the five regions is well below 20%. A current UNDP report also emphasizes the dramatic conditions in North Albania: The percentage of people on state welfare in comparison to the total population, is estimated at 44.9% for Shkodra, at 45.3% for Dibra and at 56.6% for Kukes (as at 2001; Kukes MDG, 2004, p.22). The financial support is usually very low, in most cases only 25€ per month. Having additional money from casual work or from remittances, sent by family members from abroad, is absolutely necessary to survive under the present circumstances.

All the indicators above point out the socio-economic underdevelopment of North Albania. The reasons for leaving this part of the country are found mainly among the push factors, i.e. bad living conditions and perspectives. Such a background gives a certain understanding that the willingness to migrate is still very high among the North Albanian population. Surveys carried out in autumn 2004[17] found a potential to migrate between 46% (Dibra) and almost 60% (Tropoja; see Figure 2.2). The demographic process of depopulation is still far from over and is very likely to intensify even more in the future.

---

[17] All references to North Albania are primarily based on the results of the following project: "North Albania - the emptying of a region", which was carried out in 2004 under the direction of the author, financially supported by the DAAD (pact for stability in South East Europe) (see Göler, 2005c).

Figure 2.2: Migration Potential in Selected Districts in Northern Albania.

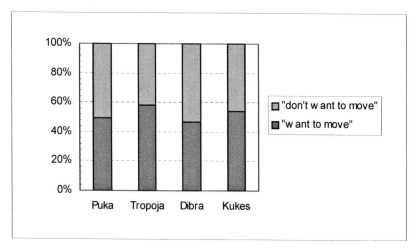

Source: Own survey from October 2004; n = 506

A parallel process to the one above is the differentiation between the regions. The population development in some selected settlements in the Tropoja district clearly shows that depopulation usually starts in peripheral mountain villages (Table 2.4). Some smaller settlements in the North Albanian Alpes are already abandonned, others are not far away from being entirely deserted like some villages in the almost inaccessible region around the middle Drin reservoir (Puka and Tropoja district) that have lost more than 50% of their population between 1995 and 2002. Another settlement type that is affected by depopulation and desertion are monofunctional mining settlements; some of them were build up in the 1970s and 1980s in connection with newly opened chrome mines for example. Most of the mines have been closed during the 1990s – in some extend a side effect of the late privatization of the former state-owned mining company Albkrom (Mema, Dika 2005, p.214). The case of the now almost abandonned village Kam between Bajram Curri and Kukes (decrease of population 1995 – 2002: 95%) shows dramatically that these settlements are no longer viable without this mines.

Table 2.4: Population Change in most Depopulated Settlements in Tropoja District (1995 – 2002)

Village/town	Municipality	Population 1995	Population 2002	Pop. Change in %
Kam	Bytyc	934	43	-95,4
Reze Mali	Llugaj	521	60	-88,5
Bukove	Llugaj	555	153	-72,4
Palce	Lekbibaj	328	92	-72,0
Zherke	Bytyc	352	99	-71,9
Curraj i Eperm	Lekbibaj	741	225	-69,6
Corr-Velaj	Bytyc	380	121	-68,2
Berishe	Bytyc	479	166	-65,3
Fierze	Fierze	2521	916	-63,7
Salce	Lekbibaj	509	185	-63,7
Cerem	Margegaj	327	120	-63,3
Peraj	Lekbibaj	746	318	-57,4
Ragam	Margegaj	285	122	-57,2
Lekbibaj	Lekbibaj	999	444	-55,6
Bradoshnice	Margegaj	176	79	-55,1
Shkelzen	Tropoja Fshat	231	105	-54,5
Leniq	Bytyc	188	88	-53,2
Qerec Mulaj	Lekbibaj	286	134	-53,1
Vishoce	Bytyc	175	82	-53,1
Brise	Lekbibaj	202	95	-53,0
Zogaj	Bytyc	354	168	-52,5
Gri, Gri e Re	Bujan	839	401	-52,2
Margegaj	Margegaj	803	727	-9,5

Source: Documents of the Bajram Curri local authorities / Tropoja district

   The depopulation of mountain villages can be interpreted as a follow-up process to what has happened in the Central European Alps until the 1960s and 1970s. With some restrictions it fits in a scheme from the late 1980s: There

Lichtenberger (1979, p.408) pointed out the west-east directed displacement of typical stadiums in agricultural development on the European continent. Especially the above described type of monofunctional redundant settlements in peripheral areas shows some general parallels to very similar recent processes of abandonment in other countries in transition (Göler, 2003; Waack, 2004).

The medium-sized capital of the region, Bajram Curri, takes an ambivalent position. With a relatively constant population, 6.600 inhabitants according to official documents, interviewees at the local administration, however, support a suspected bigger population of estimated 10.000 inhabitants. There are no empty or dilapidated residential buildings in contrast to abandoned industrial properties. Similar to other North Albanian regions, these settlements are just one stage of a chain migration destined to the capital. Quite often the only reason for taking on an occupation or the successful foundation of a business is accumulating enough capital for the next step. Since migration is socially selective, the restructuring of the population causes another problem apart from a disproportionate percentage of elderly people (see INSTAT, 2004): The exodus of entrepreneurs and businessmen, who managed to be economically successful even under the difficult circumstances in North Albania, is perhaps the most serious form of brain drain.

Demographic emptying is not the only aspect that supports the thesis of marginalisation and peripherisation of the North Albanian Highlands, as stated at above, but it is also defined by a lack of economic integration. Contrary to the Tirana conurbation, Albania's peripheries have not experienced the creation of acceptable new jobs, e.g. in the manufacturing sector after having lost their former livelihood. The high percentage of jobs in the agricultural sector (up to almost 70%) stands for the backwardness, particularly because in most cases people cannot make a living out of it.

The supposed distance to the centre (from Bajram Curri to Tirana it is only 250 km), as well as the selective loss of population are not enough to explain backwardness and missing integration. The decisive factor seems to be the absolutely insufficient supply of infrastructure. It concerns the connection to the national and international traffic network – it is a day trip to the capital –

and roads in the region itself are in very bad conditions. It also concerns the unreliable water and electricity supply that is often available only for a few hours a day or sometimes not at all, and in particular telecommunications. Under these conditions an endogenous development is far from likely and there is even nothing to attract industries, not even the job-processing ones.

The conclusion concerning regional development problems in northern Albania as a whole looks like a vicious circle, that consists of the following constituents and that will lead to further peripherisation:

- (selective) migration as mass phenomenon
- small (and decreasing) entrepreneurial basis
- poor infrastructure (electricity and water supply; road system etc.)
- sub-standard living conditions in peripheral highlands
- lack of individual living perspective

2.5   Theoretical Categorization and Evaluation from a Geographical Perspective

2.5.1   The Theory of Spatial Fragmentation...

The theory of fragmented global development (Scholz, 2002) presents a promising approach to geographical research that point out clearly the divergent ways of spatial development which have been stated and analysed in the presented contribution. The theory applies to the worldwide networks of decision-making and dependence that are organized according to market-economy and capitalism (i.e. the system usually known as globalization and that very much restricts national politics). According to the model there are three spatial categories with different degrees of dependence and integration. Putting a spatial unit into one of the three categories means to outline its part in the globalization process: "Global places" represent the global centres of political power and control. They have the necessary advanced knowledge (i.e. research and development capacities). "Globalised places" are also well-integrated. As "islands of wealth" they are economically prospering centres mostly in otherwise underprivileged developing and fast-developing countries. Their status may be defined by standardized high-tech industries or by simple job-processing industries which use the low wages to maximize their profits. Globalized places are quite often locations of natural resources with global importance. The "remaining rest of the world", left for the third category, is separated from every economic integration and the increasing wealth. With good reason this type is called "the new South" because the spatial model of global fragmentation takes up concepts of former development research and continues with the main ideas of marginalisation and social exclusion. The main difference is that there is no longer only a distinction on a global level between industrial and developing countries, but increasingly also on a regional and local level, as shown in the case of Albania.

2.5.2   ... and the Transferability to Albania

In the Albanian context the spatial patterns of the process of fragmentation can be empirically demonstrated on two levels: Most striking on the regional level is the differentiation between a single boom region and many stagnating regions. According to the theory of fragmentation this booming areas are economically prosperous, where an accumulation of capital takes place, due to specific positive conditions. In the case of Tirana this relative attractiveness mainly results from the availability of jobs and from a relatively high standard of living (as a result of the jobs, of course), compared to other parts of the country. The stagnating regions are almost unable to make any profit from these tendencies so they are often characterized by re- or degressive developments (shrinking regions) and quite the reverse happens: as new peripheries, they gradually lose touch with the global trends. That is obviously the case with parts of the Albanian periphery.

The second aspect is about the local level where spatial fragmentation is perhaps even more evident: The focus lies on rapidly growing agglomerations, e.g. Tirana, in developing and fast-developing countries. The

Albanian capital has one of the world's highest annual growth rates (Aliaj et al., 2005, p.85). And like in other urban areas with similar developments, polarisation has reached an extreme level. Fragmented urban structures become visible in marginal settlements – examples of which are also found in Tirana (Deeker et al., 2005; also see chapter 2.4.1) – as well as in separated residential areas of the upper class, known as gated communities. Following the thesis of Szelenyi (1996), all the signs that the post-socialist transformation of urban structures show are both convergence to western patterns and general tendencies known from metropolises in developing countries. In the course of these general and current developments increasing spatial disparities are to be expected in South East Europe.

2.5.3 The Significance and Evaluation of Integration and Peripherisation

According to what has just been said, Albania is currently faced with enormous problems of regional development. Not only has it got a low socio-economic level and national product (per head) when compared to other countries on the Western Balkans, but also the problem of significant and growing regional disparities. Processes of integration, on the one hand, are opposed by further peripherisation on the other hand. Other European nations, including the candidates to join the EU, are faced with similar problems, but not at the same severe level as Albania. If a future membership was to be pursued with vigour, the question rises, whether diverging spatial developments are going to become a serious obstacle to this ambition. The regional disparities in Albania must be seen as a problem for the long-term goal EU-membership because presently already 37% of the EU-budget is spent on regional structural funds (Vorauer-Mischer, 2004, p.4). And the willingness to put even more pressure on the structural support by adding further potential "eternal patients" – Schröder (2004) uses this terminus for the Italian Mezzogiorno – is decreasing constantly under the present circumstances: The current discussion around the new EU-constitution, a document that lays down mutual support by cohesion funds, is just one example.

The European or rather the German support (particularly within the framework of the "Stability Pact for South Eastern Europe" and the development cooperation of the GTZ) has sensibly set itself the goal to defuse these problems right at the beginning of membership talks. But two factors, inherent to the system, seem to stand in the way of this undertaking: That is, on the one hand, the restricted influence of governance. When looking at the relative attractiveness of the Tirana agglomeration today it is rather unlikely to delegate external investors to peripheral regions, even with investment incentives particularly for these areas (and decision-makers in North Albania are doubtful about the political will to do so). Quite the reverse, it is likely that changes of the geopolitical situation in Southeast Europe or other eastern neighbors of the EU will also have effects on the capital-extensive outsourcing industries. Since they are not bound to their location they might move their production centres to other nations with similar positive locational conditions.

Another problem, and from a present point of view a more crucial one, is that gaining further spread effects right from the beginning of any form of integration is very unlikely to be successful. As shown before the job-processing-industries are almost isolated from the national economy. Even in the immediate vicinity of their locations no backward or forward linkages of some importance have developed. And the spreading into more peripheral regions of Albania is prevented by infrastructural problems. Therefore freezing the current situation in the near future, i.e. on the level of the present disparities, would be already a success for Albania.

2.6. Conclusion

As stated at the beginning, the prospects for the countries of the Western Balkans doubtlessly are with the EU. In terms of trade connections, the integration of Albania is a de facto reality anyway: With 75% of all imports and

90% of the exports the EU-countries are the main trade partners (European Commission, 2004, p.44). Other factors like the enormous negative balance of trade may be in the way of further integration. And as long as the continuing integration and economic growth of the Tirana conurbation has no positive effects on other parts of the country, the regional disparities also have to be counted as obstacles to further integration of the whole country. To fight the further peripherisation of certain regions on the Western Balkans, implementation and the institutional establishment of regional cooperations is absolutely crucial (Altmann, 2003b). In an area that consists of many small states it is the only way to achieve the necessary economies of scale (Meurs, 2003, p.38). By following the path of establishing stronger linkages, that have their starting points in a few growth areas, the integration of peripheries could be achieved.

Bibliography

ALIAJ, B., LULO, K., AND MYFTIU, G. (2003): Tirana, the Challenge of Urban Development, Tirana.

ALTMANN, F.-L. (2003A): Die EU-Südosterweiterung. In: Meier, Christian, Pleines, Heiko, Schröder, Hans-Henning (Eds.): Ökonomie – Kultur – Politik. Transformationsprozesse in Osteuropa. Festschrift für Hans-Hermann Höhmann, Analysen zur Kultur und Gesellschaft im östlichen Europa, Vol. 15. Bremen, pp. 175-184.

ALTMANN, F.-L. (2003B): Regionale Kooperationen in Südosteuropa, Politik und Zeitgeschichte, 10-11/2003, pp.27-33.

BECKER, H., AND GÖLER, D. (2000): Stadtstruktureller Wandel in Albanien. Der Transformationsprozess im konsumorientierten Dienstleistungssektor, Europa Regional 8 (1), pp. 2-21.

BECKER, H., GÖLER, D., BERXHOLI, A., DOKA, D., KARAGUNI, M., YZEIRI, E. (2002): Transformation industrieller Standorte in der Stadtregion Tirana (Albanien), Europa Regional, 10 (1), pp. 2-10.

BECKER, H., BLÖCHL, A., DOKA, D., GÖLER, D., KARAGUNI, M., KÖPPEN, B., AND MAI, R. (2005): Industriesquatter in Tirana, Europa Regional, 13(1), pp. 12-20. (in print).

BECKER, H., FRIEMER, M., AND GÖLER, D. (2005): Stadtgeographische Veränderungsprozesse in Südosteuropa – Wohnungsmarkt und City-bildung in Tirana/Albanien, In: Mitteilungen der Fränkischen Geographischen Gesellschaft, (in print).

BURDACK, J., AND RUDOLPH, R. (2001): Post-sozialistische Stadtentwicklung zwischen nachholender Modernisierung und eigenem Weg, Geographica Helvetica 56 (4), pp. 261-273.

COMMISSION OF THE EUROPEAN COMMUNITIES (2005): Third Progress Report on Cohesion: Towards a new Partnership for Growth, Jobs and Co-hesion, http://europa.eu.int/comm/regional_policy/sources/docoffic/official/reports/pdf/interim3/com(2005)192full_en.pdf. Brussels.

DOBRINSKY, R. (2001): Multi-Speed Transitions and Multi-Speed Integration in Europe: Recent Economic Developments in the Balkans, In: Petrakos, George, Totev, Stoyan (Eds.), The Development of the Balkan Region, Aldershot/Burlington, pp. 67-74.

DOKA, D. (2001): Wirtschaftsräumliche Entwicklungen in Albanien nach de Wende. In: Lienau, Cay (Eds.), Raumstrukturen und Grenzen in Südosteuropa, Südosteuropa-Jahrbuch, Vol. 32. München, pp. 333-343.

DOKA, D. (2003). Probleme der Außen- und Binnenmigration Albaniens. In: Jordan, Peter et al. (Eds.), Albanien. Geographie – Historische Anthropologie – Geschichte – Kultur – Postkommunistische Transformation, Österreichische Osthefte Sonderband 17, Wien i.a., pp. 43-59.

EUROPEAN COMMISSION (2004): The Western Balkans in Transition, Enlargement Papers 24, Brussels.

FRIEMER, M. (2004): Wohnen in Tirana. Ausgewählte Aspekte eines Wohnungsmarktes in der Transformation, Unpublished diploma-thesis, University of Bamberg.

GÖLER, D. (2003):Raumstruktureller Wandel im sibirisch-fernöstlichen Norden. Regionale Fragmentierung der nördlichen Peripherie Russlands, Geographische Rundschau 55 (12), 26-33.

GÖLER, D. (2005a) Migration in Albanien – Tendenzen und raumstrukturelle Folgen. In: Swiaczny, Frank, Haug, Sonja (Eds.), Migration in Europa, Materialien zur Bevölkerungswissenschaft. Wiesbaden, pp. 119-132.

GÖLER, D. (ED.) (2005b): Europäische Entleerungsräume. Anwendungsorientierte Regionalforschung in peripheren Problemgebieten – Die Beispiele Nordalbanien und Oberfranken-Ost, Studime Gjeografike, Tirana/Albanien, (forthcoming).

KOROVILAS, J. P. (1999): The Albanian Economy in Transition: the Role of Remittances and Pyramid Investment Schemes. In: Post-Communist Economies 11, 3, pp. 399-415.

HATZIPROKOPIOU, P. (2005): Immigrants from Balkan Countries in Greece: Local and Transnational Processes of Incorporation in Thessaloniki. In: Belgeo, Vol. 5, No.1-2, pp. 163-174.

HELLER, W., DOKA, D., BERXHOLI, A. (2004): Hoffnungsträger Tirana. Abwanderung in die Hauptstadt Albaniens, Geographische Rundschau 56 (1), 50-57.

INSTAT (2002): The Population of Albania – Main Results of the Population and Housing Census, Tirana.

INSTAT (2004): Migration in Albania, 2001 Population and Housing Census. Tirana.

KASER, K. (2002): Dörfer in der Krise. In: Kaser, Karl, Pichler, Robert, Schwandner-Sievers, Stephanie (Eds.), Die weite Welt und das Dorf. Albanische Emigration am Ende des 20. Jahrhunderts, Wien/Köln/Weimar, pp. 162-187.

KING, R. (2004): Albania: Interrelationships between Population, Poverty, Development, Internal and International Migration, Mediterranee 3.4, pp.37-47.

LAWSON, C., SALTMARSHE, D. (2000): Security and Economic Transition: Evidence from North Albania, Europe-Asia Studies 52 (1), pp.133-148.

LICHTENBERGER, E. (1979): Die Sukzession von der Agrar- zur Freizeit-
gesellschaft in den Hochgebirgen Europas. In: Haimayer, Peter,
Meusburger, Peter, Penz, Hugo (Eds.), Fragen geographischer
Forschung. Festschrift des Instituts für Geographie zum 60. Geburtstag
von Adolf Leidlmair, Innsbrucker Geographische Studien, Vol. 5.
Innsbruck, pp. 401-436.

MEURS, W. VAN (2003): Den Balkan integrieren. Die europäische Perspektive
der Region nach 2004. In: Aus Politik und Zeitgeschichte 10-11/2003,
pp. 34-39.

MEMA, F. AND DIKA, I. (2005): Privatization and Post-Privatization in Albania:
A Long and Difficult Path. In: Kusic, S. (Edt.): Path-Dependency in the
Western Balkans - The Impact of Privatization, Frankfurt, pp. 193-220.

PETRAKOS, G., AND TOTEV, S. (2001): Economic Performance and Structure in
the Balkan Region. In: Petrakos, George, Totev, Stoyan (Eds.),
Development of the Balkan Region. Aldershot/Burlington, pp. 3ff

RUß, W. (1979): Der Entwicklungsweg Albaniens. Ein Beitrag zum Konzept
autozentrierter Entwicklung, Transfines, Studien zu Politik und
Gesellschaft des Auslandes, Meisenheim am Glan.

SCHOLZ, F. (2002): Die Theorie der „fragmentierten Entwicklung", Geographische Rundschau 54 (10).

SCHOLZ, F. (2004): Geographische Entwicklungsforschung, Studienbücher der
Geographie, Berlin/Stuttgart.

SCHÖNFELDER, B. (1999): Wirtschaftsstrukturen. In: Hatschikjan, M. A. (Ed.), Südosteuropa – Gesellschaft, Politik, Wirtschaft, Kultur, München, pp. 325-346.

SCHRÖDER, F. (2004): Mezzogiorno. Der ewige Patient, Geographische Rundschau 56 (5), pp. 30-37.

STADELBAUER, J. (2000): Räumliche Transformationsprozesse und Aufgaben geographischer Transformationsforschung, Europa Regional 8 (3-4), pp.60-71.

SZELENYI, I. (1996): Cities under Socialism – and after. In: Andrusz, Grgory, Harloe, Michael, Szelenyi, Ivan (Eds.), Cities after Socialism. Urban and Regional Change and Conflict in Post-Socialist Societies, Oxford/ Cambridge, pp. 286-317.

UNITED NATIONS ALBANIA (2004): Kukes MDG. Regional Development Strategy, available at www.undp.org.al/?elib,576, (19.04.2005).

VORAUER-MISCHER, K. (2004): Regionen der EU. Problemgebiete und Regionalförderung, Geographische Rundschau 56 (5), pp. 4-9.

WAACK, C. (2004): Ländliche Peripherien im Kontext der EU-Erweiterung, Europa Regional 12 (2), pp. 92-99.

Chapter 3

Vedran Horvat:

Circulation of Intellectual Capital in South-Eastern Europe – Assuring Transition

3.1 Abstract

Forced migrations that occurred in the past decade in the Balkan region had an impact on the labour market in the countries of the European Union. Except for the low skilled workers, well known as typical immigrants from the 60's and 70's, young and educated experts appeared to emigrate to the West at the beginning of the 90's, showing the outflow of intellectual capital due to war and gross human rights deprivation. With the current stabilisation of the region, there are still some questions which remain open. High potential of human capital in the region is highly unutilised and therefore isolated from the global labour market. The emigrants as the carriers of expertise, but also of culture of living in a democratic environment are rarely contacted in order to boost and improve the quality of transition of their home countries. Reforms which characterise the transition process require professionalism and expertise and most of the countries in the region have great difficulties to conduct them, what hinders the process of EU integration. Countries in South East Europe dispose valuable human resources which show a high level of flexibility and efficiency in countries where freedom, meritocracy and creativity are stimulated and evaluated. Therefore, an innovative strategy for acquiring sustainability through adequate distribution and management of human resources; their mobility and circulation within the region, could improve the conditions for EU-integration.

3.2   Introduction

Wars and conflicts that appeared on the Balkan landscape during the 90's followed by various forms of deconstruction of existing social forms and gross violations of human rights opened up a new era of migratory movements in the South Eastern Europe region. While migrants during past periods (from the early 60's to late 80's) were mainly low skilled workers pushed by their wish for a higher standard of living, a migrant picture in the 90's offers another, much more complex perspective. War events tackled each social group and caused some kind of a migratory movement. Among the hundreds of thousands of emigrants and refugees which have been re-located from their domestic environments (usually it meant home countries) there were many high skilled persons; scientists, experts, intellectuals and artists. In addition to that, there was a significant number of persons that flew before events that had to come. But also there were persons that stayed in their home countries during the war and made a decision to emigrate after its end. Briefly, intellectual capital of the region was also significantly devastated due to the war since a serious number of highly qualified persons flew and found their new professional environments in the large number of European countries, U.S.A., Canada or Australia – that are even today the most attractive destinations of HSP's (high skilled persons).

This paper underlies the notion that both, the quality and speed of transition – which is today an inherent element of two basic processes: globalisation and EU integration - are determined by the number and active enrolment of high skilled individuals with expertise in a multitude of fields and with intercultural competences. However, their high potential is still highly unutilised and therefore, in significant extent, isolated from the global labour market. The emigrants as the carriers of expertise, but also of culture of living in a democratic environment are rarely contacted in order to boost and improve the quality of transition of their home countries, mostly because they are substituted with less educated persons, inclined to civic servility. Reforms which characterise a transition process require professionalism and expertise and most of the countries in the region have great difficulties to conduct them, what does not just hinder the process of EU integration, but threatens the sustainability of the region as a whole.

In addition, the need for the active civic engagement of 'the best and the brightest' is still highly underestimated in the regional environment; burdened with notions of nepotism and corruption. Those who are forming a new generation of a high and educated elite, are often inclined to leave the country because they are attracted by a host country that offers a living and working environment which will be able to utilise their full potential and offer them conditions which they perceive as adequate to their skills and knowledge. This is combined with the lack of interest of state institutions to absorb the most qualified persons; they rather use those who are politically more adequate, what is still a residuum which has not been erased by transition. Unfortunately, also the civil societies of involved countries do not show the capacity to accumulate human capital and to produce conditions which could be functioning as pressure-factories for the state institutions which are ought to carry the process of transition.

3.3   Circulation of Intellectual Capital

Under-utilisation and low circulation of high skilled persons within the educational, scientific and business institutions in the region is a direct consequence of devastated national economies that lost trust and have uncompleted processes of reconciliation between the states involved. The process of scientific exchange is still poorly addressed and reduced to rare examples supported mostly by subjects of the international community. Thus providing particular and to purpose reduced 'know how' which can be addressed from a critical perspective, especially toward so-called international community (IC) transfer of knowledge. However, one should be worried because of the lack of awareness in domestic institutions and at decision-making points in the governments in the region. Orientation toward joining the EU, with right 'cost-benefit' studies, is surely giving the right direction to a broader region. However, this can not be the only instrument to raise the role of education and science in the country with the goal to achieve both sustainability and stability, especially in the circumstances when investments in education cannot be compared to an average in the EU countries.

In some countries within the region (like Croatia and Bulgaria), more concrete and partially successful steps have been recently made in order to counter negative effects of "brain drain". They managed to transform it to a phenomenon with a positive label, to "brain circulation" – that is inherent to experts, scientists, intellectuals and other high skilled individuals – from more developed countries, some even in Central and Eastern Europe (Baltic states, Slovenia, Czech Republic). "Brain circulation" mostly consists of short-term migration between involved countries but can also be perceived as the pattern of socialisation of (young) scientists and intellectuals that share joint life-styles. This process has to be continued in the following decade in order to create conditions that are favourable for the mobility of high skilled persons within the region, since most of them are attracted by opportunities in the EU, U.S. etc. Therefore, as most propulsive societal sectors in the context of EU integration, both science and education (and consequently culture) can play a pivotal role in the integration process. Due to these reasons, mobility and circulation of high skilled individuals, as the agents of the integration process within the region (in science, education, economy and civil society sectors), are of crucial importance. Why ? Because these are sectors which are not just most integrated in the global processes but also possess a critical and objective approach, intrinsic to scientists. But what is even more important is that a significant part of that elite is capable to reflect meritocratic principles which imply individual responsibility and boost the competitiveness which can naturally improve the quality of transition by self-selection processes.

Given that the "brain circulation" phenomenon depends largely on the political and economic environment of the particular country, and taking into account that none of the governments is actually interested to boost the development of knowledge-based society alone, a regional perspective (in terms of exchange and cooperation) should be considered. This can offer a lot, especially if the regional cooperation considers countries on a similar stage of development as parties among which 'brain circulation' is possible to appear.

However, in countries like Macedonia, Bosnia Hercegovina and Albania, "brain drain" is still of great volume, and, if we let alone the few incentives from the civil sector emerging from IGO's incentives, it significantly disables successful transition (and consequently integration). Social change that occurs due to negative effects of emigration of high skilled people is more and more evident since it decreases the level of professionalism in the society, and consequently, threatens the whole process of transition, leading the region in a sphere of uncertainty and instability. On the contrary, if high skilled persons would be absorbed and adequately managed by state institutions, the private sector and the civil society could produce a shift toward a sustainable society in a certain period of time. However, due to the high level of emigration during the last decade[18], most of the high skilled potential of the region is already relocated and resides in a transnational sphere of mobility. There are countries in South East Europe that dispose valuable human resources which show a high level of flexibility and efficiency to where freedom, meritocracy and creativity are stimulated and properly evaluated. Therefore, an innovative strategy for acquiring sustainability through adequate distribution and management of human resources (their mobility and circulation within the region) could improve the conditions for integration with the EU.

It is anyhow encouraging that the ex patriated nationals are recently more and more organized in networks. Networking can be defined as "a mode of interaction" and can take many forms: interpersonal interaction, organisational contacts and internetworking.[19] Along with the development of communication technologies (mostly Internet) as the new instrument of integration with global science and economy in last decade, the so-called 'scientific diaspora networks' appeared. Since these individuals have already been inserted in the new professional environments, evaluated according to

---

[18] According to estimations that significantly vary and suffer from the lack of data, in the last decade, a few hundred thousand highly educated people flew out of the SEE region. Among them were 15 to 20. 000 experts, scientists and Ph.D. holders.

[19] Stone, D. (2000): Think Tanks Across Nations: The New Networks of Knowledge, http://www.nira.go.jp/publ/review/2000winter/07stone.pdf.

their merits and achievements, they can provide an example of good practice and foster the transfer of knowledge to their own home countries through more intensive scientific and cultural exchange. Furthermore, they are the real bearers of the social knowledge inherent to the European Union, since they are, at an individual level already an integrated part of the region within the EU and carriers of cultural memo, needed for transition. Therefore, those 'expatriated' can be an asset for the origin country and far from being loss (as it was perceived until recently) if it creates and applies strategies to influence the decision-makers. The concept of social capital helps us to understand what kind of effective involvement in the development of the country these potential diaspora networks can have.[20] This notion is in fact not supported by a number of scholars (Gaillard A.M., Meyer J.B. and Brown, M.) that claim that it is unlikely that many of the expatriates will return because they settled and built their new professional environments. Thus, it remains open for each of the home countries to find and lance innovative strategies of how to use their 'know how' for the development of their home country.

'Social capital also plays a relevant role in the potential for brain gain. Although people decide to move for better opportunities, they retain connections and networks back to their home country. When these networks are fostered they can yield a flow back of knowledge and new technologies. The important advances in communication technology may limit the extent to which skills are actually lost.'[21] Meyer and Brown point out that intellectual/scientific diaspora networks have as a specific purpose impact on the development of the origin country. They state that these networks 'are heavily reliant on the Internet and engage in various joint developmental projects with government agencies, private and non-profit organizations at home. The actions they stress, consist mainly of research projects, technology transfer and expert consulting, training courses and bringing foreign based companies in their home country'[22]. This

---

[20] Panescu, C.A. (2004): A New Perspectives of Highly Skilled Migration, Diplomatic Academy, Ministry of Foreign Affairs, Bucharest, p.3

[21] OECD (2001), International Mobility of the Highly Skilled, OECD, Paris

[22] Meyer, J.B.; Brown M. (1999): Scientific Diasporas: New Approach to the Brain Drain, MOST

supports the thesis that this particular region can benefit from the alleged negative migratory movement. Nevertheless, a strong critical perspective has to be taken into account here, since high skilled persons are social agents who would have to provide long-term self-sustainability and not long-term dependence on foreign investments.

3.4 (Un)sustainable Countries and Transition to EU

This perspective is much more important for the region than it seems at first. Having in mind a narrow and old-fashioned interpretation of the demand and supply mechanisms and transcending this framework, a broader understanding would lead decision makers in the region to utilise the human potential as the most important resource which is able to integrate their societies through culture, education and science – as most propulsive and contributive societal sectors. This is an inevitable process and the SEE region has to raise consciousness about the resources which could be utilised by the EU, but also has to determine the strategy to achieve the own and long-term sustainability which has been seriously threatened, let alone now (nationalistic) "loss-of-sovereignty" concepts of accusations.

The European Union is aware of the fact that "in the context of growing global competition for highly skilled research staff, it should attract (young) research talents from all over the world. Therefore, in addition to offering an excellent research environment, obstacles to entry and mobility within the EU should be removed."[23] This official statement could be an invitation and warning at the same time for the region; first to those who are aware that they can negotiate with their own competitiveness and show competence with their own skills and knowledge; and second, for those who will be perceived as the poor, 'good' managed by demands of labour market and therefore utilised in narrow economical terms.

---

[23] 'Conclusions and Recommendations of the EU-Conference (2004): Brain Gain – the Instruments, The Hague, NUFFIC conference

Furthermore, the strongest argument that speaks on behalf of detrimental effects of high skilled emigration is the negative impact on transition, due to the lack of skilful, fresh and innovative representatives of new social elites, capable to boost the transition.

However, this effect could also be minimised by ensuring their participation in their home country's development, while they reside in their host-countries. It goes without saying that countries with a higher level of democratic consolidation and with more success in economic transition are inclined to be affected to a lower extent by high skilled emigration than those which are still fragile and unstable. Reasonably, the individuals from the latter countries will have more reasons to leave the country; firstly due to the uncertainty and deprivation, and secondly due to the goal of decovering a healthier, more creative and liberate working environment if they are in the position to compete with their own skills or expertise.

But again, although it does address international mobility as contributing to development, the EU declares that measures have to be taken to limit the negative impacts of brain drain from those less developed, particularly vulnerable countries. This notion surely does include the Western Balkan region and gains weight if we look up the recent recommendations of the EU-Conference "Brain Gain – the Instruments" held in the Netherlands in the year 2004. To become the world's most competitive and dynamic knowledge-based society, Europe needs to raise its number of highly qualified researchers significantly. To achieve this goal, the European Commission has estimated that roughly 700.000 additional researchers are deemed necessary to attain the 3% Barcelona objective and that European education institutions will not be able to deliver all of them.[24] Therefore, it is natural that they will search for them in the neighbourhood.

The brain drain is now characterised by a demand-pull on the side of the receiving countries, of which the immigration policies are reflecting domestic labour-market shortages. Combined with traditional self-selection effects on the

---

[24] Conclusions and Recommendations of the EU-Conference (2004): Brain Gain – the Instruments, The Hague, NUFFIC conference.

supply side, this leads to much higher migration rates among the highly educated and increases transfers of human capital from developing to developed countries.[25] And right there, a big space for intervention of decision-makers throughout the region is opened: to create conditions for experts, scientists and intellectuals, to establish regional centres of excellence and think tanks that could utilise the knowledge in policy-making processes and build the requirements for 'brain circulation' in the region. Briefly, with proper timing and adequate measures (introducing bilateral agreements and immigration quotas), countries in the Western Balkans could take the chance to educate their students and at the same time enable them to be present and attracted by the domestic institutions. Such incentives, to encourage the establishment of various inter-disciplinary institutes and think tanks that could continuously produce positive impacts on the countries development should certainly be followed by state incentives. Up-to-date, such incentives are rare cases and still mostly depend on state funding, what significantly reduces the scope of their influence.

'The importance of policies (national and regional) to control the movement of skilled migrants has escalated'[26] recently, becoming a possible threat to the right of free movement in the contemporary world. After 11/9/2001 and terrorist attacks that followed, it is expectable that some basic human freedoms will be threatened, due to the fear from terrorism. But still, one can share the Iredale's perspective that 'skilled migration is not going to diminish, and restrictive or punitive attempts by source countries to prevent losses are likely to fail.'[27]

Meyer and Brown stated that until the late 1980's, national and international policies focused on both preventive and regulative measures that were thoroughly studied. However, they stress that they failed to bring feasible

---

[25] Panescu, C.A. (2004): New Perspectives of Highly Skilled Migration, Diplomatic Academy, Ministry of Foreign Affairs, Bucharest, p.2.

[26] Iredale, R. (1998): The Analysis of Factors Generating International Migration, Technical UN Symposium on International Migration and Development, The Hague, Netherlands.

[27] Iredale, R.: The Analysis of Factors Generating International Migration.

or effective solutions, mostly because there were wrong underpinnings with theoretical assumptions based on 'human capital' approach.[28] International meetings and initiatives in the past few years (ECA/IDRC/IOM (2000); OECD (2001), ILO/DFID (2001)) opened ground for revision of traditional brain drain/human capital-based approaches (restriction, repatriation, compensation)[29], followed by tailoring the temporary entry policies by many governments in order to attract highly-skilled professionals or to encourage the return of skilled nationals from overseas.[30]

Ouaked (2002) offers an interesting perspective according to which 'long-term strategies to promote economic growth are needed to enable developing countries to retain and draw back their highly skilled and address the negative effects of the brain drain. Migrants themselves can play an important role through their remittances, diaspora networks and own willingness to return - at least temporarily - to share their skills and contribute towards economic progress.'[31] But still, economic growth and development, important for the country's sustainability, are not prior to the overall role of scientists, intellectuals and artists in a society. Their contribution to the society, especially

---

[28] Meyer, J.-B. and Brown, M. (1999): Scientific diasporas: A New Approach to the Brain Drain, prepared for the World Conference on Science, UNESCO-ICSU, Budapest,

(Two ways to counter the loss of human capital is either to restrict the flows through authoritative decisions or to evaluate its monetary cost and get financial compensation.).

[29] Meyer, J.-B.: Network Approach versus Brain Drain, p.104.

[30] Iredale, R. (2002): The Migration of Professionals: Theories and Typologies, p. 4 ('Taiwan has progressed farthest down the 'return migration' and much of the economic miracle of Taiwan is attributed to the government's success in encouraging professionals to return home').

[31] Ouaked, S. (2002): Transatlantic roundtable on high-skilled migration....,p.164.

See also: 'Education, training and targeted economic development may actually increase skilled migration in the short-to-medium term, but it is the best means of addressing developing country skill shortages over the long run. The promotion of human rights may also play a role in this context.' In: Findlay, Allan. M and Lowell, Lindsay B. (2001): Migration of Highly Skilled Persons from Developing Countries: Impact and Policy Responses, Report prepared for the ILO, Geneva.

in South East Europe, should be perceived far beyond classical, neo-liberal concepts of country development.

Iredale suggests that "sending countries" may consider encouraging or supporting their high skilled population to take part in "brain of circulation" instead of trying to block them. This must be accompanied by long-term policies designed to assure the country's development. In this sense, "brain circulation" can be utilised for the purposes of updating both technology and management in the fields that are prioritised by these policies. Simultaneously, their advanced students or already migrated high skilled nationals should be both invited for frequent exchanges by sponsored temporary visits and participating in related projects at home. Policies that have been mentioned need to be followed with an improvement of the political, social and economic environment in the country.[32]

3.5 Knowledge-based Societies – an (un)real Option for Western Balkans?

According to Iredale, this strategy has two goals; the acceleration of "brain circulation" of high skilled persons in the light of the development of national interests and in the context of globalisation and optimisation of their contributions to those interests regardless of their country of residence. Sending countries may also try to improve their home environment in order to attract HSP's from other countries to work in those areas prioritised in the national development plan, if they are existing. Surely, this strategy may challenge certain political and cultural interests in the countries involved.

'Governments may play a positive or negative role in influencing incentives for highly skilled workers to stay or move abroad. They may play a positive role by providing incentives for foreign skills to flow in or remain in the country for instance by facilitating immigration by less work permission restrictions, providing tax incentives and promoting the country as an attractive

---

[32] Cao, X.: Debating 'brain drain' in the context of globalisation, Vol 26.

working and living environment.'[33] Surely, it would contribute to the development of a more pluralistic, healthier and knowledge-based society which can develop on the basis of the prosperity of included diversities.

Gaillard explains that 'there are definitely no quick fixes to stop brain-drains because success depends very much on the level of the economic, scientific and technological development of each country and on the political leaders taking a long-term view of the whole thing.'[34]Although countries in SEE are still mostly 'sending' countries, it is likely that some of them will soon become the 'receiving' countries, which can imply the appearance of 'brain circulation' form migration. These countries[35], also called 'buffer zone countries', will probably become interesting for immigrants from distant places because they are placed along the EU border and they will have to cope with significantly higher numbers of migrants than it was the case until now.'[36]

Immigration to the EU is likely to increase in the near future, as a result of both demand for labour and low birth rates in the EU. In the short and medium term, many of these requirements are likely to be met by flows from Eastern Europe, particularly following the eastward enlargement of the EU. The newest tendency in the European Union, to allow skilled immigration to occur in a legal and much facilitated form, is likely to be efficient in the 'battle' for the 'best and brightest'.[37] Nevertheless, mostly due to unemployment and

---

[33] Mahroum S.: Europe and the Immigration of Highly Skilled Labour, p.29, see also: Mahroum, Sami: Highly-skilled globetrotters: mapping the international migration of human capital', London, R&D Management, 23-31.

[34] Gaillard, A.-M. (2001): Brain Drain to Brain Gain.

[35] From the same reasons Slovenia was from 1995-2002 under strong and massive immigration flows of asylum seekers. Now it is characterised as immigration country. It is likely that Croatia will also share the similar situation; the number of residence permits issued in last few years is continuously increasing.

[36] Laczko, F., Stacher, I. and Klekowski von Koppenfels, A. (ed) (2003): New Challenges for Migration Policy in CEE, IOM and ICMPD, Hague. (Labour migration in CEE countries)

[37] Mahroum S., 'Europe and the Immigration of Highly Skilled Labour', in International Migration of the Highly Skilled, (ed. by Robyn Iredale and Reginald Appleyard), International Migration

terrorism, fear and reluctance have also arisen in Europe, regarding absorption/integration of foreigners and immigrants in their own societal sectors. In spite of that, together with Straubhaar, one can conclude that high skilled immigration to EU countries appears as an inevitable part of the enlargement processes. Those high skilled nationals from new member countries, but also present candidate countries, will play a significant role in fulfilling the gaps in their labour shortages. Reaching the goal of a strong European Research Area is hardly achievable without considering the presence of HSP's from EU neighbour countries. Anyhow, applying this perspective, fragile and developing transition countries from SEE would have to apply innovative strategies to offer their 'skills and knowledge' on the global market, at the same time fostering the transfer of 'know-how' to their domestic environments. But the EU itself still has to recognise and to channel the distinction between the two emerged worlds. One is led by the vision of scientists, experts and artists dedicated to their disciplines and arts, which already reside in transnational, united and integrated spheres of the European Union, where SEE already is part of the larger virtual scientific and cultural community. The other world, led by the political elite which is sometimes inclined to instrumentalise science, culture and art for narrow political purposes, is still atomised according to the nation-state interests that determine the rules of the labour markets, influence immigration and security laws, all significantly reducing human rights, freedom of expression and consequently – freedom of movement – which is implied as necessary for the everyday activity of all scientists, experts and artists.

Journal, VOL.39 (5), p.28 (It must be emphasized here that it is a significant shift to more liberal immigration policy) Examples: France introduced so-called 'scientific visa' as a fast track procedure to allow scientists from countries in the non-European Economic Area (EEA) to work in France. It is well known that Germany in 2000. also introduced 'green cards' for IT professionals from non-EEA countries. Netherlands and Sweden also provide tax discounts for highly skilled foreign personnel.

Bibliography

CAO, X. (1996): Debating 'Brain Drain' in the Context of Globalisation, A Journal of Comparative Education.

Conclusions and Recommendations of the EU-Conference (2004): "Brain Gain – the Instruments", The Hague, NUFFIC conference.

FINDLAY, A. M. AND LOWELL, L. B. (2001): Migration of Highly Skilled Persons from Developing Countries: Impact and Policy Responses, Report prepared for the International Labour Office (ILO), Geneva.

IREDALE, R. (1998): The Analysis of Factors Generating International Migration, Technical UN Symposium on International Migration and Development, The Hague, Netherlands.

IREDALE, R. (2001): The Migration of Professionals: Theories and Typologies, in: International Migration of the Highly Skilled, (ed. by Robyn Iredale and Reginald Appleyard), International Migration Journal, VOL.39 (5).

LACZKO, F., STACHER, I., AND KLEKOWSKI VON KOPPENFELS, A. (ED) (2003): New Challenges for Migration Policy in CEE, IOM and ICMPD, The Hague.

MAHROUM, S. (2001): Europe and the Immigration of Highly Skilled Labour, in: International Migration of the Highly Skilled, (ed. by Robyn Iredale and Reginald Appleyard), International Migration Journal, VOL.39 (5).

MAHROUM, S. (2000): Highly Skilled Globetrotters: Mapping the International Migration of Human Capital, R&D Management, Vol. 30. /1 Blackwell, Oxford.

MEYER, J.-B. AND BROWN, M. (1999): Scientific Diasporas: A New Approach to the Brain Drain, prepared for the World Conference on Science, UNESCO - ICSU, Budapest.

MEYER, J.-B. (2001): Network Approach versus Brain Drain: Lessons from the Diaspora, in: International Migration, Vol. 39 (5).

OECD, POLICY BRIEF, (2002): International Mobility of the Highly Skilled, OECD Observer

PANESCU, C.A. (2004): A New Perspective of Highly Skilled Migration, Diplomatic Academy, Ministry of Foreign Affairs, Bucharest.

QUAKED, S. (2002): Transatlantic Roundtable on High-Skilled Migration and Sending Countries Issues, International Migration, Vol. 40 (4).

STONE, D. (2000): Think Tanks Across Nations: The New Networks of Knowledge, http://www.nira.go.jp/publ/review/2000winter/07stone.pdf.

Chapter 4

Isa Mulaj:

Trade Performance and Foreign Direct Investment in Kosovo during the United Nations Administration as the Determinants of a Distinctive Path of Transition towards the European Union

4.1   Introduction

Not only the UN administered economy of Kosovo is much different from the rest of the Western Balkan countries, but it has also some economic paradoxes. Over the last six years, Kosovo received substantial international assistance to revitalize its devastated economy and to make a transition towards economic integration with the European Union (EU) membership being the ultimate target. There is no doubt that the progress has been remarkable in economic reconstruction. Meanwhile, with the international assistance of donor type being reduced substantially, prospects for a sustainable economic development from own resources remain bleak, at least in the short run. Chances to fill the gap through attraction of foreign direct investment (FDI) have been hindered, among others, by the unresolved political status. Greater inflow of FDI is expected in the course of privatization which is still underway, though the process has a long way to go to its completion. While FDI is seen as a source of triggering greater economic vitality, the paradox is that even domestic resources available, especially financial ones, are not being used properly or to the extent they could be. Some domestic funds find it easier to be used and capitalized abroad. Furthermore, it is surprising how the small budget of Kosovo recorded surplus at the end of fiscal years 2001 to 2003, leaving some deficiencies in the quality of services to be delivered to those who contributed to it, and by the end of 2004 the budget suddenly turned into deficit.

The future of the small economy of Kosovo depends also on trade policies, economic cooperation with the neighboring countries and the EU's integration programs and initiatives. Kosovo's main trading partners are Albania and successor states of former Yugoslavia or the Western Balkans. Imports are several times higher than exports causing a huge trade deficit. This disproportion is partially a result of trade liberalization and limited competitiveness of the emerging economy. In spite of these disadvantages which may delay the journey towards the EU, Kosovo has got some comparative advantages vis-à-vis the Western Balkans to be closer to that integration. Some of the standards required as a prerequisite for membership in the EU are already in place such as: access to Kosovo by foreigners is almost free (no visas are required), the legal framework is in full accordance with the EU standards and all the regulations are available in English, foreign companies are fully free to repatriate their profits and Euro is the official currency in use.

The aim of this paper is to investigate and find where Kosovo stands in the path towards the EU by bringing together path-advantages and disadvantages, with a focus on trade performance and FDI analysis. To start with such an investigation, in section one we provide an overview of Kosovo's economic transition. Section two assesses trade regime and foreign trade. It shows that apart from foreign aid and remittances, Kosovo's economy remains heavily dependent on imports, and that the implication of the trade deficit (both in aggregate terms and in most of the products) puts Kosovo in almost total economic dependence from abroad. Differently from import dependence, FDI as an alternative of substituting a part of the imports are not only small, but actually there is not any assessment of their effects. We have tried to shed some light on this issue in section three. After getting insights on these aspects of Kosovo's economy, the task in section four was to elaborate and discover Kosovo's economic integration perspectives and challenges in Southeastern Europe (SEE) and the EU. The last section concludes and addresses few policy recommendations.

4.2 An Overview of Kosovo's Economic Transition

The break-up of the former Yugoslav federation that began in 1991 with the independence of northern republics – Slovenia and Croatia – continued with the separation of Macedonia, the war in Bosnia and Hercegovina – BiH (1992 to 1995) – and the war in Kosovo (1999) and resulted in a complete disintegration of the former Yugoslav market into republics and regions. Many business networks that Kosovo had with them and foreign countries collapsed, bringing an economic downturn which, when measured in terms of GDP per capita in 1995 of $400, was less than 50% of the 1989 level (World Bank, 2000). This is an event to remember because when it comes to necessity of repositioning in the market, successor states of former Yugoslavia, in particular those bordering Kosovo, emerged as the main trading partners, thus showing a similar pattern as in the past. However, this pattern in newly created circumstances is facing various obstacles hindering better economic cooperation and integration. An international administration (United Nations Interim Administration in Kosovo – UNMIK) was established since June 1999 with a mandate, among others, to administer and facilitate Kosovo's transition process and future political status.

After a decade of neglect and consequences of the war in 1999, many were surprised how the economy of Kosovo was reviving quickly. In the first two years, private sector activities began growing rapidly under legal and regulatory vacuum. Much of that was a continuation of the activities of private enterprises established during the 1990s and/or those that had their origin in self-management socialism.[38] Inherited poor infrastructure was substantially improved during the emergency phase of reconstruction from 1999 to 2002 by

---

[38] The scope of private sector activities during self-management socialism in former Yugoslavia (in which Kosovo was part of) was greater than in any other socialist country. The 1974 Constitution of former Yugoslavia and of Kosovo allowed the so-called 'small economy' where private businesses of a family-owned type could employ up to a maximum of 10 workers (depending on the type of activity). Private sector in agriculture was even of greater importance. Peasants were allowed to hold up to 10 hectares of land per household and that made nearly 90% of land area in Kosovo being in private ownership.

investments of the international donors. But since the end of the emergency phase of reconstruction there was a lack of a strategy as how to proceed with a sustainable economic development. To what the international community did not pay proper attention after reconstruction, was the problem of financing and maintaining the systems in which it has invested. That is why some segments of infrastructure are decapitalizing (European Stability Initiative, 2004). Nowadays more than six years after the UN administration, the economic and social situation of Kosovo is still fragile. In the first two years after the war of 1999 the people of Kosovo were the most optimistic in the world with respect to expecting a better economic future (Index Kosova, 2002), their perceptions about the present remained pessimist whenever asked. Faced with the fact that massive unemployment and widespread poverty which they observed cannot be reduced significantly in the near future, the overwhelming majority of them steadily felt dissatisfied about the economic situation.[39]

Kosovo is a small country covering an area of 10,887 km^2, in which around 2 million inhabitants live with an estimated GDP per capita of €1,300 (as estimated by the International Monetary Fund for 2004). At the first glance this may suggest that the level of economic development has been significantly improved not only compared to the years of sharp decline during the 1990s, but also to a better state during self-management socialism until 1989. If one looks into more detail one can, realize that Kosovo's economy suffers from macroeconomic distortions whereas positive economic growth is not expected until 2006. Table 4.1 summarizes basic macroeconomic indicators and their change since 2002.

---

[39] A public opinion poll of 1,262 respondents of Kosovo over March 2003 to November 2004 by quarters revealed the following trend and level of dissatisfaction with the economic situation: in 2003 - March 67.7%, July 65.0%, November 71.8%; and in 2004 – March 75.3%, July 70.7%, November 67.7% (UNDP, 2004).

Table 4.1: Kosovo's Macroeconomic Indicators

(in millions of Euros unless otherwise indicated)

	2002	2003	2004	2005[a]	2006[a]
GDP	2,447	2,426	2,516	2,433	2,428
Consumption	2,623	2,600	2,699	2,626	2,597
Investment	603	572	591	599	623
Government expenditures	402	543	749	746	736
Net export (Ex – Im)	-779	-746	-774	-793	-792
➢ Exports	321	300	298	301	308
➢ Imports	1,100	1,046	1,072	1,094	1,100
Current account balance	-880	-745	-733	-700	-666
GPD per capita in €	1,235	1,256	1,301	1,263	1,256
GDP growth (annual)	-2.9%	-1.1%	-3.7%	-0.5%	2.6%
Government revenues (% of GDP)	28.8	32.8	31.9	30.8	-
Total budget	500	590	601	614	625
Bank deposits	413	501	395[b]	-	-
Foreign assistance	887	688	573	514	487
Unemployment [c]	47.2%	44.4%	n/a	-	-
Number of registered job-seekers [c]	257,505	280,923	300.697	-	-

[a] International Monetary Fund – IMF projections.

[b] Banking and Payment Authority of Kosovo (2005), Monthly Statistics Bulletin No. 41, January 2005, Prishtina.

[c] World Bank (2005), Kosovo Poverty Assessment: Promoting Opportunity, Security and Participation for All, Report No. 32378-XK (June), Poverty Reduction and Economic Management Unit of the World Bank, Washington D.C.

Source: IMF (2005), Aide Memories of the IMF Staff Mission to Kosovo, April 20th to May 4th, 2005, IMF, Washington D.C.

Assessments of GDP should be taken with great caution as they vary and are inconsistent not only between different institutions but also within the same institution for the same year. For example, the report of IMF Staff Visit to Kosovo of March 10-19, 2004 put the following assessments for GDP: €1,522 million for 2002, €1,580 million for 2003, and €1,641 million for 2004 (very much different from the assessments in the report of the forthcoming year or the figures presented in the Table above). A report of the World Bank (2005) indicates that GDP growth in Kosovo was positive over 2002 to 2004 (3.9% in 2002, 4.7% in 2003 and 6.5% in 2004) which is different from assessments of the IMF that showed negative growth over the same period. Although one may not be sure which estimates may correspond to the state of the facts, the differences suggest that inaccurate and inconsistent measures of macroeconomic indicators in Kosovo remain a problem for decision-making, design and implementation of macroeconomic policies. Obviously, everyone is aware of this disadvantage but more serious attention should be in place.

Referring to the figures in Table 4.1, Kosovo's GDP trend was to some extent dependent on the gradual decline of foreign assistance. Consumption as one of the components of GDP which always appears to be higher than the GDP itself includes a considerable amount of remittances by Kosovo emigrants working abroad (more on this later). There are other problems which show Kosovo's weak economy such as: very low level of export, small share of investment to GDP, high unemployment (ranging from 30% to 40%) and above all, widespread poverty.[40] Hopes to reduce these problems significantly in short to medium term without involving substantial resources from abroad and intensive use of those at home would be unrealistic. But Kosovo's economic problem is not so much or entirely, as the International Crisis Group – ICG (2001) thought, related to its weak domestic capacity. It may be to some extent as Mack (2003) came to a conclusion that Kosovo's economic capacities are not weak but hidden. In a similar language for the Western Balkans, Barret (2002) maintained that there are many development opportunities that are not properly investigated and utilized. This is what the IMF (2002) recommended for Kosovo as a goal to develop domestic productive capacities in terms of economic policies in the near future.

---

[40] As of 2002, the measures of poverty level through the Household Budget Survey showed that 37% of Kosovo's population live in poverty (spending less than €1.42/day per adult) and 15.2% were in extreme (food) poverty (consuming less than €0.93/day per individual) (Statistical Office of Kosovo, 2003).

4.3 Kosovo's Trade Regime and Foreign Trade

Once semi-closed during the 1990s, the economy of Kosovo emerged as fully liberal and open in the first decade of the 21st century. The lack of products and services for immediate needs of the population and requirements for reconstruction of the war torn society imposed openness. A massive influx of goods supplied by donor communities, importers and exporters characterized Kosovo in the second half of 1999. At that time, as UNMIK was in the phase of supporting the establishment of provisional institutions of self-government of Kosovo or joint interim administration structure, it needed resources which initially came from the donors and later from the collection of taxes. The regulation on the establishment of an institution that would be in charge of overall financial management of the Kosovo budget, design of fiscal strategy, taxation system and macroeconomic conditions, was passed on November 1999 (Regulation of UNMIK No. 1999/16 on the Establishment of the Central Fiscal Authority of Kosovo and Other Related Matters). Before that, UNMIK passed the Regulation On the Establishment of the Customs and Other Related Services in Kosovo (on August 31st, 1999) and the Regulation on the Currency Permitted to be Used in Kosovo (on September 2nd, 1999). It then followed several regulations passed during 2000 to regulate economic, fiscal and trade issues of Kosovo. This legal framework made the Central Fiscal Authority operational which became the cornerstone of the Ministry of Economy and Finance of the Government of Kosovo after general and parliamentary elections in 2002.

Much of the framework regulating fiscal and trade affairs have undergone changes but their discussion would go beyond the scope of this paper. Not surprisingly, businesses began to complain about tax charges, especially against border taxes on raw material and equipment. A survey by Riinvest (2001) of 300 private enterprises showed that over half of them considered taxes and customs duties as too high, though in reality they were not higher than in the neighbouring countries. Tax administration was justifying the tax system in place with the reason that the needs of Kosovo's budget for revenues can be first of all fulfilled by border taxes charged against largely import oriented business communities. Concerns of businesses that they are heavy taxed have been lowered by extending taxation base to personal income tax (20%), profit tax (20%) and property tax (0.05%) that made budget revenues more spread (in 2000 around 95% of Kosovo's budget revenues were financed by taxes charged against businesses).

Without going into more details about the taxation system and fiscal policy, the current trade regime of Kosovo consists of: i) 0% VAT on exported goods (no customs duties); ii) a tariff rate of 10% charged at the border for all imported goods except those subject to excise taxes which have different higher rates or per value; iii) VAT of 15% as a border tax for imported goods. These tax rates do not apply to all countries that Kosovo has trade exchange with. Goods coming from Macedonia are not subject to customs duties at the border (only VAT is collected) except a charge of 1% of goods' value collected in the name of customs' fees. Trade with Serbia and Montenegro (SM) is free, probably because Kosovo is still considered as a part of the union SM. A Free trade agreement has been signed with Albania in July 2003 and entered into force in October of the same year. Ideally, Kosovo does not seem to have impediments to trade with the neighboring countries, but the following sub-section finds a number of barriers to trade.

4.3.1   Exports and Imports: From an Aid-based to a heavily Import-Oriented Economy

Kosovo's exports to other countries were always small. Nearly 2/3 of trade by destination in 1987 was delivered to the local market, with some 1/4 being delivered to republics of former Yugoslavia. Only around 12% of total trade amounted as export to other countries (Uvalic, 2004). Majority of that export was carried out by the socially-owned enterprises (SOEs) operating in the industrial sector. Despite the fact that the structure of exports was not so favorable because mainly intermediary products, electricity and raw materials were exported, again it was important for Kosovo's economy. Now that most

SOEs in collapse have lost their markets and are undergoing privatization, newly established private enterprises which in general are of small size (employing on average less than 10 workers per company) and being specialized, have started to increase their volume of export but still not being able to follow the growth rate of goods coming in. The table below shows the situation in more details.

Table 4.2: Trade Exchange of Kosovo with Other Countries (by years in €)

Countries	Exports		Imports		Trade balance	
	2002	2004	2002	2004	2002	2004
Albania	1,359,194	2,682,364	48,039,917	31,241,316	-46,680,723	-28,558,952
BiH	600,349	1,516,302	13,487,994	11,988,454	-12,887,645	-10,472,152
Croatia	2,705,974	633,175	23,276,824	21,897,722	-20,570,850	-21,264,547
Macedonia	3,384,119	9,311,793	145,678,934	161,167,422	-142,294,815	-151,855,629
SM	4,613,758	5,739,934	232,642,302	170,648,952	-228,028,544	-164,909,018
Western Balkans	12,663,394	19,883,568	463,125,971	396,943,866	-450,462,577	-377,060,298
Italy	7,522,851	6,156,323	26,747,601	41,399,511	-19,224,750	-35,243,188
Germany	2,461,554	3,133,280	34,336,107	71,906,285	-31,874,553	-68,773,005
Greece	199,070	4,630,813	55,763,737	78,756,947	-55,564,667	-74,126,134
Other EU	971,988	2,531,226	115,451,081	111,325,222	-114,479,093	-108,793,996
Total EU	11,155,463	16,451,642	232,298,526	303,387,965	-221,143,063	-286,936,323
Turkey	1,160,056	2,969,626	76,392,538	80,588,844	-75,232,482	-77,619,218
Suisse	42,536	158,433	19,049,613	18,163,695	-19,007,077	-18,005,262
Other	2,275,959	5,645,833	127,655,283	231,125,705	-125,379,324	-225,479,872
TOTAL	27,297,408	45,109,102	918,521,931	1,030,210,075	-891,224,523	-985,100,973

Source: Trade Exchange of Kosovo (2004), Ministry of Trade and Industry of the Government of Kosovo, Prishtina, 2004, Table 4.2 and author's own calculations.

Apart from massive international aid as a part of the reconstruction program, large quantities of imports were mainly financed by previous savings of the local businesses and the population as well as by remittances of Kosovar emigrants. The figures presented in Table 4.2 are published by the Ministry of Trade and Industry which have been provided from UNMIK's customs service or the official data. They do not include informal trade and smuggling which we may assume to be very large in Kosovo.[41] In any case, the official figures show that Kosovo's main trading partners are its neighboring countries due to geographical proximity and trade regime that we referred to earlier. Geographical proximity may also explain trade cooperation with Greece as one of the main trading partners from the EU, but not with Germany and Italy, probably because of the impact of their larger economies on trade.

The EU Council Regulation 2007/2000 which has entered into force in 2000 recognized Kosovo as a special region giving it trade preferences. Kosovo's trade benefits so far under these preferences have been below expectations, probably because of geographical distance which incurs higher transaction costs. Should Germany and Italy be closer to Kosovo, trade benefits would be greater. Let alone proximity, export opportunities to the EU are facing another obstacle – standardization of products at the EU requirements.

Kosovo's trade exchange has continuously led to deepening of its trade deficit. This does not recommend that Kosovo has to be more protectionist. On the contrary, the future of its small economy, as Michalopoulos (2003) argued, will depend on foreign trade. But right now, Kosovo is at a disadvantaged political situation (unresolved political status) to make sure that its liberal trade regime is not abused by other countries, especially its neighbors. Preferential treatment of Macedonia to trade in Kosovo granted by UNMIK is being used by other countries to falsify the label of their products as originating from Macedonia.[42]

A closer look of Kosovo's trade exchange by the type of products also shows trade deficits in almost all of them (as presented in Table 4.3). All these

---

[41] There is not any approximate measure about the size and share of informal sector to Kosovo's GDP. In the neighboring countries in 2003, the share of informal sector to GDP was estimated to have been as follows: Albania (35.2%), Macedonia (36.3%) and Serbia and Montenegro (39.1%) (Schneider, 2004). Given that these countries are Kosovo's main trading partners, the share of informal sector to Kosovo's GDP should not be expected to be lower than 40%.

[42] This is similar to illegal trade in SEE which Holzner and Gligorov (2004) present as being carried out through fake invoicing. The most frequent products in faked invoicing are: petroleum, cigarettes and cars. All countries of the Western Balkans are strongly involved in fake invoicing.

indicate an unfavorable competitive position of Kosovo which has complicated trade deficit (more on that in the forthcoming sub-section). Of course, no country in the modern world is independent in the sense of being able to provide all resources, goods and services without entering in trade relations with other countries. If it is not possible to reverse the deficit of some products, at least it is possible to diminish their large dependence. Metal scraps and items, various intermediaries, beverages, textile and plastic products dominating the small volume of export, are some of Kosovo's options to diminish import dependence.

Table 4.3: Exports and Imports of Kosovo by Type of Products

by years in €	Exports		Import		Coverage of imports by exports (%)	
Products	2003	2004	2003	2004	2003	2004
Vegetable products	1,858,728	255,671	64,301,476	70,416,697	2.9	0.4
Foodstuffs, beverages and tobacco	529,0511	3,589,070	197,170,208	166,213,445	2.7	2.2
Mineral products	0	2,094,194	133,502,962	152,185,765	0.0	1.4
Chemical and industrial products	669,880	1,014,937	67,190,954	98,278,534	1.1	1.0
Plastics and associated products	2,225,022	2,804,210	30,549,465	41,666,818	7.3	6.7
Raw hides and skins	3,206,325	6,342,976	205,712	966,195	1559	656.5
Textiles and textile items	1,590,494	1,359,265	12,142,116	30,899,353	13.1	4.4
Metal scraps and items	10,643,618	19,266,625	52,748,414	77,125,555	20.2	25.0
Machinery and mechanical appliances	4,142,408	1,766,826	90,563,326	108,892,506	4.6	1.6
Miscellaneous manufact. goods	5,725,849	827,951	65,606,862	46,026,162	8.7	1.8
Other	1,892,182	5,787,377	256,957,440	237,539,045	0.7	2.4
Total	37,245,017	45,109,102	970,938,935	1,030,210,075	3.8	4.4

Source: Trade Exchange of Kosovo (2004), Ministry of Trade and Industry of the Government of Kosovo, Prishtina, 2004, Table4.2 and author's own calculations.

Exports of some machinery and mechanical appliances that appear in Table 4.3 are the products which are exported to Kosovo first, then re-exported. Small volume and the share of agricultural products exported which in 2004 has fallen, may leave the impression that Kosovo is still not able to satisfy its needs even within an inch. Here the problem is not so much related to inability of satisfying the needs, but to agricultural products being exported to Kosovo from the countries which subsidize them. Given the liberal trade regime of Kosovo and the import of agricultural products which are tax exempt, then foreign subsidized products become cheaper than those of Kosovo that do not enjoy subsidies. Most farmers and consumers in Kosovo rightly complain that it is not worthy to produce when costs outweigh benefits, i.e. it is cheaper to buy it ready rather than to produce it. In this domain, trade liberalization has its costs in driving home producers out of business. This is where Kosovo should either consider a degree of protectionism (e.g. introducing import quotas) or support agricultural development.

There is another product not presented here which Kosova used to export a lot in the past – electricity. Electricity is too essential in modern economy. Kosovo's vast resources of coal (which in former Yugoslavia accounted for around 50% of the total) made many experts, including the World Bank, come to a conclusion and recommend that Kosovo in the future can be the source of power supply to the countries nearby. Without taking into consideration environmental consequences that arise from electricity generation in thermo power stations, Kosovo has got a real opportunity to use electricity as one of its main economic engine. Putting aside this perspective in the future, the irony is that in spite of this potential Kosovo at present continues to suffer from electricity shortages. Large amounts of investments made in Power Corporation of Kosovo (KEK) after the war estimated at around €700 millions, mainly from the European Agency for Reconstruction (EAR) were not successful in providing uninterrupted power supply. Clearly, the problem is in managing this horizontally integrated corporation for which the Kosovo Trust Agency – KTA (an agency established to privatize SOEs and restructure enterprises in public ownership such as KEK) is in charge. Privatization of SOEs and their restructuring is Kosovo's other potential source to boost export.

In addition to limitations and obstacles to export that we superficially discussed here, it is important to analyze obstacles faced by those who export. Exporters first of all complain about a lack of credit support, which in part may be attributed to the lack of subsidies for some group products such as those of agriculture. Most of the barriers to export presented below may be summarized as being related to the government policies and deficiencies of the trade regime with other countries.

Table 4.4: Barriers to Export as Perceived by a Sample of 110 Kosovar Exporters

Type of barriers	Intensity indicator
Lack of credit support	71.6
Customs tariffs of other countries	66.3
Delays at border crossings	57.0
Lack of travel documents and visas	46.6
Trade regime with other countries	45.2
Lack of information on export markets	43.6
Difficulty to find business partners	35.7
Bad image of Kosovo products	33.9
High manufacturing costs	33.6
Shipment costs	31.4

Source: Riinvest (2003), Trade Policies and Export Promotion in Kosova, International Round-
    table Forum (November), Riinvest, Prishtina.

Customs tariffs of other countries (Kosovo has 0% VAT on exported products) and delays at border crossings are common barriers faced by exporters of the neighboring countries too, though the lack of travel documents - passports and visas is a specific barrier faced by Kosovar exporters. This in turn has made exporters reasonably to emphasize other related barriers such as the lack of information on export markets and the difficulty to find business partners. UNMIK has tried to resolve the problem of passports by issuing provisional documents to travel abroad, but some countries still do not recognize them. Had Kosovo's political status been resolved, these specific barriers probably would not exist. The barrier named as 'shipment costs' is worth explaining. Kosovo's exports (and also imports) are charged with transit charges of 3% in Serbia and 5% in Montenegro, whereas Kosovo's infrastructure may be used by everyone free of charge (UNMIK, 2004). Such an asymmetric trade relation has become an obstacle to economic cooperation and integration between these small countries which in the map still appear as a single state.

4.3.2   Trade Deficit and its Implications on Structural Distortions

One of the major problems and challenges of Kosovo's economy in general and economic policies in particular, is how to reduce large trade deficits arising from heavy reliance on imports, by increasing domestic economic growth and export. While no one is expecting to change that course soon because of the constraints mentioned in the previous sub-section, there are some good preconditions which, if used in a smarter way, gradually may lead to an increase in Kosovo's competitiveness. In this sub-section we first describe implications of the trade deficit, then try to find out and discuss some inroads for reducing it.

The figures in Table 4.1 show that Kosovo's trade deficit is higher than the total budget. Since the largest amount of budget revenues according to the Ministry of Economy and Finance (2005) are collected at the border or taxes on imports (68%) and given that consumption goods dominate the structure of Kosovo's imports, then Kosovo's population somehow appears to be a working class and consumption society, the money of which largely ends up abroad. The loss of a part of budget revenues due to asymmetric trade relations with the neighboring countries is generating advantages for them to export to Kosovo and deepening its trade deficit. The risk is that as long as this trend continues, it may damage the budget and bring the economy in a vicious circle of economic stagnation with a tendency to decline.

Huge trade deficit and structural distortions also characterized other countries during their emerging transition but did not last longer than in Kosovo. Under political *status quo*, this deficit will persist and become a serious obstacle for macroeconomic stability and economic growth, because,

Kosovo is an unequal trade partner in foreign trade and its hands right now are somehow tied to do anything more. Regardless of the crucial importance of final political status and who will be in charge to make major decisions, there are several possible ways of how to reduce the trade deficit. The first way is to redefine trade relations with the neighboring countries on the basis of trade reciprocity principles. That would enable Kosovo to have greater access to foreign markets and increase exports after Serbia and Montenegro would have removed their transit charges. Redefinition with Macedonia implies a more rigorous control by Kosovar as well as Macedonian authorities of the origin of the products being exported to Kosovo. If that is to function properly and efficiently, it would lead to the growth of Kosovo's budget revenues through the taxation of foreign products which currently enter with the label of Macedonia to avoid customs duties. The benefits would not end only in more budget revenues. Domestic firms would benefit from being more equal with foreign competitors whose products now would be more expensive as a result of border taxes. Such measures would give rise to more business transactions at home and could provide the basis for increasing domestic capacities for which there are many objections that their current low level is a disadvantage to provide sustainable economic development. Another way to compensate the costs of imports and to reduce the trade deficit is to attract FDI, which we explore in the following section.

4.4   Foreign Direct Investment

Since the beginning of transition in Central and Eastern Europe (CEE), FDI appears as a significant source contributing to economic development. The magnitude and the impact of FDI inflow in CEE is heavily attributed to various factors and transition policies implemented such as: geographical zone, political and economic stability, the state of infrastructure, methods of privatization, purchasing power of the population, trade openness and accession to the EU (Bos and van de Laar, 2004). The origin of FDIs in CEE is largely from the EU countries and can be explained by geographical proximity, trade liberalization in order to attract FDI and transition of CEE countries towards EU membership. However, the dynamics of inflow and growth level of FDI across CEE has been non-homogeneous because of transition-specific factors (Carstensen and Toubal, 2004). Among several important determinants of attracting FDI, Campos and Kinoshita (2003) listed: institutions, rule of law, low labor costs, abundance of natural resources, trade openness and liberalization and close proximity to the major developed countries. FDI in transition economies of the Western Balkans were lower than in the CEE because of higher political risk and uncertainty caused by warfare, intrastate or inter-ethnic tensions (Brada et al., 2004). Country's initial conditions were also considered to be as a determinant to attract FDI, though there is no sufficient evidence in support of them, except the fact that during turmoil, institutional and physical insecurity, FDI will be missing. This was the case in Croatia, BiH, and Serbia due to high risk during the 1990s (warfare, political isolation, UN sanctions). But FDI inflows which brought significant improvements in the manufacturing sector in other CEE countries were not as expected, even in Slovenia as a politically stable country (Damian and Majcen, 2001). In Macedonia, after independence, there were little FDI until 1998 when they started to increase significantly (Slaveski and Nedanovski, 2002).

Following this basic theoretical framework we may start analyzing FDI in Kosovo. To begin with initial conditions, i.e. after the war of 1999, many potential foreign investors visited Kosovo to search their opportunities to invest. Much more interest was shown by Kosovar emigrants who for a long time could not return to Kosovo. They were interested in Greenfield investments and/or partnerships with local firms. As they observed that stabilization of Kosovo required more time than they had thought (institution building, rule of law, infrastructure development), their enthusiasm began to shrink. At that time there were no apparent FDI whereas Kosovo was being flooded by imports; therefore foreign investors were still observing the situation and opportunities to invest later. The first FDI with greater importance that could be noticed in post-war Kosovo were those in the financial sector or in the establishment of banks and institutions of micro-finance.[43]

Now that institutions and legislation are in place, the inflow and the role of FDI in Kosovo are still unknown. The assessments of the IMF (2005) that in 2004 the FDI inflow was only €2 million and that the same amount was projected for 2005, are inaccurate and unrealistic. The share of FDI per capita in Kosovo is not known, because the assessments of GDP and FDI are inconsistent and far from accuracy. It is true that Kosovo as a part of the Western Balkans is characterized by investment risks and high costs of inadequate infrastructure (Hunya, 2004), but it is unlikely that FDI are so low, regardless other risks. Political risk, that is considered to be one of the main obstacles, existed in BiH too, a country with 4.2 million inhabitants, but FDI totaled to $380 million (Kekic, 2004) there in 2003. Due to the lack of any appropriate data for analysis, the following part of this section will discuss prospects and challenges to attract FDI in Kosovo.

Political risk may not be a major obstacle to foreign investors as they would not care much about the final political status of Kosovo. What they are more concerned about is an appropriate business environment. Power shortages and unfair or informal competition are the main obstacles as they increase operation costs and reduce competitiveness (World Bank, 2004). The impact of these obstacles is undermining Kosovo's great trade openness as one of the main determinants of greater inflow of FDI. Trade patterns too, which, as we observed earlier, are being carried out with the neighboring countries that are small and with a low level of development, have not resulted in FDI inflow whatsoever. It follows that geographical proximity in attracting FDI does not matter much among less developed countries. Trade patterns seem to matter

---

[43] The first two largest private banks established in Kosovo after the war were: ProCredit Bank (initially known as Micro Enterprise Bank) established with the capital of Commerzbank in Frankfurt; and Raiffeisen Bank Kosovo (which is a successor of the former American Bank of Kosovo which Raiffeisen bought out). FDI in the financial sector in Kosovo can be explained by two main factors: i) hard currency in use (Euro); and ii) financial assets are easier and faster to be taken away in the case of unexpected risks.

quite a lot between a developing and the developed country(ies) in FDI inflow towards the poorer. Looking back at Table 4.2 we see that Kosovo also carried a great deal of trade with Germany, Italy and Turkey. A study of Riinvest (2002) based on a survey of 38 foreign-owned companies found that the companies from these countries lead in FDI to Kosovo.

Differently from many transition countries where management and employee buy-outs are used intensively as the primary method of privatization that deterred foreign investors, the method of privatization in Kosovo is exclusively chosen to attract FDI. The sale of SOEs to domestic and foreign buyers through spin-offs is the main method of privatization being implemented in Kosovo. At the beginning of the privatization process in Kosovo which commenced in the second half of 2003, foreign investors did not get involved as expected, most likely due to many complications, including political and legal confusions that led to the suspension of the process in October 2003 after two waves of privatization that included some 20 companies (Mulaj, 2005). Privatization of SOEs restarted after a year when it was suspended and now has entered a progressive phase with over 100 SOEs privatized (around 20% of the total) by the end of 2005. Two large SOEs acquired by foreign investors in 2005 through special spin-off privatization included: Ferronikel – iron ore and mining, that was sold to the British based company Alferon for €33 million (the buyer is required and pledged to invest €20 million and employ 1,000 workers), Llamkos – factory of galvanized sheets was sold to the Bulgarian steel producer Kremikovtsi for € 4,152,250 which promised to invest €15 million and employ 500 workers in the forthcoming two years.[44]

---

[44] Alferon was declared the winner of Ferronikel in the second round of bidding after the KTA cancelled the provisional winner in the first round, the Albanian-American company Adi-Nikel, which had offered a higher price (€49 million). The sale of Llamkos is concluded despite suspicions of collusion among the bidders. Many were surprised of the very low bid price (slightly above 1 million Euros) that Ispat-Mittal Steel Holding (member of LNM Group, the largest steel producer in the world) offered for Llamkos in the first round of bidding. It withdrew from bidding in the

Of special importance not only in terms of FDI but also for overall economic development of Kosovo have been and still are, the remittances of Kosovar emigrants. There is no estimation about Kosovar emigrants living and/or working aboard, though it is assumed that this number may be around 500,000 or 25% of Kosovo's total population mostly in Western Europe with Germany accounting for the largest number. Emigration due to hard economic conditions always characterized Kosovo. Much of today's Kosovars abroad are the people who moved out there during the Serbian rule in the 1990s where economic conditions for a part of the population came to the limits of economic existence. Remittances at that time were mainly used for consumption needs and maintain some sort of economic activity to survive.

The analysis of the role of remittances in economic development recently has attracted attention especially in developing countries. Gross remittances to developing countries are on the rise but their effect on macroeconomic performance is still a subject of debate and empirical analysis of their determinants of inflow remains very limited. This is because, as Lucas (2005) identifies and which is relevant for Kosovo, the evidence is largely based on household surveys. Among very scarce analysis about the impact of remittances in Kosovo, a survey of Riinvest (1999) found that they go more for consumption and less for investment. Beginning with the principle that consumption generates production which in turn is related to investment, the impact of remittances in consumption is seen as a source of development. That is how it is supposed to work in theory but not so much in reality of Kosovo. As we repeatedly stated, Kosovo's consumption goods are mainly imported, thus remittances for this purpose go abroad and encourage production and investment there, or in the countries that export consumption goods to Kosovo.[45]

Like other economic indicators, estimates about remittances coming to Kosovo are approximate. The amount of remittances in 2004 varied from €340

---

second round leaving Kremikovtsi the only bidder. In less than three months after Kremikovtsi bought Llamkos, Ispat posted the news that it has successfully completed the deal for acquiring.

[45] Kremikovtsi (see: http://www.sofiaecho.com/article/ispat-buys-kremikovtsi/id_12058/catid_23)

million in the estimation of the IMF (2005) to a maximum of €500 million in the figures of the Ministry of Economy and Finance (2005). Remittances account for at least half of Kosovo's budget and their importance for the economy and the population is undisputable. Without attempting to investigate any possible better alternative use of them, we should emphasize that Kosovo has got other financial resources at disposal that are not being used adequately for the purpose which they are allocated. Kosovo's budget, as a plan of government revenues and expenditures after several years of surplus, slipped into deficit by the end of 2004 by 25% of GDP.[46] That is why the IMF is continuously warning and advising budget policy makers in Kosovo. That is only one of the stories in managing financial resources. Hundreds of millions of Euros in deposits of local banks are kept abroad. Over €100 million of the Kosovo Pension Savings Trust and over €100 other millions of Post and Telecom of Kosovo are being capitalized abroad at far lower interest rate than that in Kosovo, with a justification of a greater security abroad. Proceeds from the sale of SOEs or privatization are kept in a frozen account of the KTA. All these amounts imply an additional budget for Kosovo which, if used in Kosovo, would fill the gap of FDI. In fact, Kosovo has become an FDI outflow.

Euro as Kosovo's official currency in use has replaced former Deutschemark (DEM) in 2002. The impact of DEM in economic transactions during the 1990s was greater for Kosovo than for any other country of the Western Balkans for the following two reasons: i) remittances of Kosovar emigrants in Germany to alleviate hard economic conditions mentioned earlier; ii) hyperinflation of the Dinar during 1993 that was the second highest in the world economic history, making Kosovo Albanians lose their faith completely

---

[46] This unexpected deficit occurred within less than a month due to excessive spending of funds by some ministries and institutions after general elections in Kosovo (held in October 2004), where there were changes in the management of those ministries/institutions. One explanation for the budget surplus is that it was a result of the system on commitment basis that the budget was organized, which is different from current cash basis.

to the monetary policy of Serbia which had occupied Kosovo.[47] Now, that the risk of that sort of hyperinflation with the Euro does not exist anymore (otherwise it would mean the collapse of the EU), the question is how Kosovo can make use of this strong currency to attract FDI. The use of the Euro has brought enormous advantages since many costs are eliminated in exchange rate, provisions, transfers, etc. To see what advantages the Euro produces for Kosovo, we should first consider some of its disadvantages. To almost every Kosovar, the replacement of DEM by Euro has come with more consequences than in Germany. The first impact was through a 'shock in prices' or the rise of prices in general. The claim of many people associated by a frustration that the introduction of the Euro has kept the same numbers in prices that were in DEM is rejected. What is true is that there has been a rise in prices. For example, prices of many items that have been DEM 1 and something up to DEM 1.5 were simply rounded up to €1, even though the exchange rate at the time of replacements was DEM 1 = €0.51. Since that 'shock' has overcome, prices in Kosovo still remain high. Living in Prishtina (capital of Kosovo) is as expensive as in any other large citiy in Western Europe. However, high prices have one advantage. They normally signal foreign investors to invest in an environment where purchasing power of a part of the population is high (e.g. foreigners working for the UN in Kosovo, salaries of local people employed with international organizations, remittances of Kosovar emigrants) while local labor force is cheap like in the neighboring countries, young and relatively well-educated. Higher costs of doing business in Kosova compared to the region right now due to the constraints mentioned earlier are temporary. Kosovo has resources and good prospects to resolve them and to become competitive in the region. A small market at home imposes the need to export

---

[47] Hyperinflation in the so-called 'rump Yugoslavia' consisting of Serbia and Montenegro where Kosovo was also part, reached an annual rate of 363 quadrillion per cent in 1993. On the economic consequences of that hyperinflation, an economist from Belgrade (Jurij Bajec) said: "I hope there will be no power cuts because all Serbia's GNP is in its freezers" (The Economist, 10/9/1993, p.60).

in the neighboring and other foreign countries. That is why integration for Kosovo is necessary and unavoidable.

4.5   Kosovo's Perspective in Regional and European Integration

What comes after disintegration? Many unexpected, expected, bad and good events and finally integration. Transition associated with the break-up of former Yugoslavia led to divergent *go it alone* policies in its successor states (Bicanic, 1996). Former unified market collapsed and new trade barriers emerged. Slovenia and Croatia which traditionally were more developed were able to partially compensate the loss of former Yugoslav markets by new patterns of trade with the Western Europe. They had better connections with the Western European markets even before and geographical proximity played a role. On the other side, trade benefits they had with the rest of former Yugoslavia are not yet restored at a satisfactory level, because disintegration of former Yugoslavia is not yet over. This disintegration shall include the independence of Kosovo which will happen in the near future, and very likely the independence of Montenegro. Then integration has to evolve on a different path from that of self-management socialism associated with the slogan *brotherhood and unity*, the final result of which was slaughtering each other. Integrations that were a cause of some forces or revolutions led to disintegration (e.g. the collapse of socialist system in CEE and disintegration of former Yugoslavia). Only as independent integrations are more sustainable and natural.

Many thought that after the end of the conflict in Kosovo everything will go towards stabilization and progress. They seem not to have recognized and underestimated the complex political situation. A study conducted by Chesapeake Associates (2001) with 125 companies in Southeastern Europe (25 companies from each of the following countries: Albania, Bulgaria, Kosovo, Macedonia and Montenegro) assessing obstacles to trade, investment and regional competitiveness, showed that the companies from Kosovo ranked poor in the state of infrastructure (telecommunication network, roads, power shortages) as number 1 (in other countries this rank was 5). Kosovo's infrastructure at that time was really poor. The obstacle number 2 for Kosovo was a custom related problem which was the concern of other countries that perceived it as the most severe problem (ranked as number 1). Another common point between companies in Kosovo and those in other countries was that political risk was considered as the smallest problem (ranked at the bottom or rank 8 in both cases). This clearly contradicts many complaints about high political risk to do business in the Balkans. Nevertheless, if political risk in Kosovo at the level of individual case studies was not a problem, in general environment certainly it was. The longer the political status of Kosovo persists, the more danger it may bring to the neighbouring countries. That is why Glenny (2004) sees the long-term political solution for Kosovo as crucial for the entire region of SEE.[48] ICG (2005) recommended that by the early 2006 Kosovo should adopt a new constitution and by mid-2006 UNMIK should hand over all the power to the Kosovo Government. That would make Kosovo independent which should be recognized by the international community, though some international presence and monitoring will remain (a sort of monitoring mission and NATO's military presence).

One of the crucial components for Kosovo's economic development is the extent of openness of other economies in SEE and the initiatives of the EU in the region such as the Stability Pact established to overcome historical disputes in the Balkans (Mustafa, *et al.,* 2001). This initiative of the EU and the World's Bank SECI (Southeast European Cooperative Initiative) is an opportunity to strengthen regional cooperation between SEE countries and their institutions. The region of SEE may expect greater benefits if a good coordination between these and various initiatives is in place (World Bank, 2003). Initiatives and support from abroad are necessary for the region, but it

---

[48] Resolution of final political status of Kosovo is expected to come through negotiations (likely with Serbia) proposed by UNMIK. We should emphasize that negotiations are a step back compared to socialist era where each federal unit of former Yugoslavia had a nominal right to secede, or the right to self-determination.

would be more important that the countries of the region approach each other independently to cooperation.

Of all countries in SEE, Kosovo is in a more disadvantaged position due to its specific situation. Kosovo should get integrated within its territory at first. There are still some enclaves of Serb minority, which Kosovo alone cannot integrate. Great decision-making powers, including Russia as the ally of Serbia have made it clear that whatever the final status of Kosovo will be, it shall not include territorial secession, neither return under Serbia nor union with any other neighboring country. Therefore, as long as Serb minority continues to look towards Belgrade and receive orders from there and boycott Kosovo's institutions, integration will be delayed. A useful lesson of internal integration can be learned from Macedonia. Following the Ohrid Agreement, Albanians now are more represented in the institutions of Macedonia and look towards Skopje. A similar chance is offered to the Serbs in Kosovo by the UN; to coexist with Albanians and work together for Kosovo.

In foreign relations, Kosovo under current circumstances has made progress in trade cooperation. It is worth referring to cooperation with Albania. Relations between Kosovo and Albania in the past were restrained as a result of isolation of Albania during Enver Hoxha's regime and because of the Yugoslav policy regarding the national question of Albanians in Kosovo who might have seen Albania as their mother country. Differently from then, most Albanians in Kosovo now see the perspective with Albania in getting integrated through intensive economic cooperation and fully free trade exchange. This attitude is supported not only by the leadership but also by the majority of the population of these two countries. Such integration enables access of Kosovo to the Adriatic Sea and connections with Italy and Greece that are Kosovo's important trade partners. Good cooperation is in place with Macedonia which in turn has good relations with its neighboring Bulgaria. This way through enables Kosovo to reach Turkey or one of its major trade partners. Bulgaria is to be admitted to the EU while negotiations with Turkey have just started. Through Macedonia, Kosovo is also connected to Greece and then to the Aegean and Mediterranean Sea. Cooperation with Serbia remains undermined by political disputes between the two countries. Located to the north of Kosovo, Serbia provides good connection of Kosovo to Central Europe. In all these roads, Kosovo is a crossroad; Macedonia has the shortest way of link to Montenegro and BiH through Kosovo and the shortest way of Serbia to Albania is through Kosovo.

4.5.1   How Far or Close is Kosovo from the European Union?

Currently, no country bordering Kosovo is a member of the EU. Of all Yugoslav successor states only Slovenia has made its way through to full EU membership. Apart from Croatia that has made the needed progress to apply for membership, prospects for the rest of the Western Balkans involve two scenarios: i) Albania and Macedonia may be admitted before others; or ii) all Western Balkans will move together in that direction. The first scenario is more likely to happen first. In the second scenario we should distinguish Kosovo, the independence of which has not yet been recognized. In this sub-section we consider the current place of Kosovo in relation with the EU. Here we shall discuss a little whether Kosovo should go more to the EU or whether the EU should come to Kosovo.

The EU is already present in Kosovo since 1999. Its main task was reconstruction through various programs implemented by EAR. The so-called Pillar IV of UNMIK that is in charge of reconstruction and economic development is managed by the EU and means that the EU is managing the economy of Kosovo. According to the Commission of the European Communities (2002), the EU, by the end of 2001, has assisted Kosovo with €1,131.8 millions. Kosovo, from 2002 to 2004 has benefited from around €245 millions from the EU program called CARDS.[49] The Country Strategy Papers outlined a number of support programs for the Western Balkan countries,

---

[49] CARDS – Community Assistance for Reconstruction, Development and Stabilization has been established by the EU in December 2000 as a program under Stabilization and Association process to support the Western Balkans on their journey to the EU in various projects in reconstruction, institutional and legislative development, sustainable economic development and to promote closer relations and regional cooperation among countries and the EU (European Commission, 2004).

including, among others, enterprise development in order to generate employment (Pinto, 2004). In Kosovo such a program is in operation through Regional Enterprise Agencies.

Current political status limits Kosovo not only to become a more active participant in relation with the EU, but also constraints it to benefit from international financial organizations such as the IMF, the World Bank and International Finance Corporation. There is no doubt that quicker resolution of the final political status will open new ways to improve Kosovo's economic situation, but the people should not expect miracles. It may simply be that after independence many people will leave the country to search for better opportunities in the EU member states, which of course is in the interest of Kosovo and its population facing high unemployment and poverty. The importance of independence after all would be that it will make institutions and people feel more responsible and work harder. It will also make them independent in a sense that they will no longer have the feeling of being subordinated by someone. However, they will still need the direct support of the EU for a long time.

Membership in the EU requires a considerable number of standards to be fulfilled. We will skip elaborating Kosovo's conditions and chances of fulfilling them as this is a difficult task under current circumstances. Table 4.5 summarizes both advantages and disadvantages of Kosovo with respect to the EU integration. What is more relevant here to consider is how Kosovo and its population are in general terms to the EU, while the EU standards are a task for future research. Kosovars in general are Western oriented as a result of a considerable number of its emigrants living in the West and a number of Western organizations and personnel operating in Kosovo. Many Kosovars speak and/or use English at their working place. They also speak Serbo-Croatian, though recently this language is in decline among new generations and because of heavy dominance of English. Some Kosovars speak German which has come as a result of larger number of emigrants working abroad. German language may also be used for business between Kosovo on the one hand and German speaking countries on the other hand (Germany, Austria, Switzerland).

The presence of the EU in Kosovo should be used intensively as a unique advantage. But Kosovo needs to be integrated in the region first. Improving relations with Serbia is crucial for both sides. One may refer to a number of examples how old enemies have turned to become good partners and friends. We should mention Germany and France, which from enemies in World War II became allies after the war to initiate the establishment and represent the backbone of what today is known as the EU. This was made possible by clearing out the consequences of the past, after which there was the will and determination to move ahead towards integration. A similar example is not applicable now between Serbia and Kosovo. The will should come from Serbia after it recognizes and accepts that its policies in the past were wrong and the determination to move ahead with new integration should be common both for Serbia and Kosovo.

Table 4.5: Kosovo's Path-advantages and Disadvantages in the Prospects of EU Integration

Determinant	Path-advantages	Path-disadvantages	Comments and remarks
Geographi-cal position	Small territory in the heart of SEE and one of its major cross roads.	Relationship with Serbia still unclear and vulnerable to instability.	Good relations and connections with other countries. Better relations with Serbia are necessary for greater and easier access to Central and Western Europe.
Free access	Everyone can travel to Kosovo; no visa required	Risk from unchecked entry may make Kosovo a transit country to illegal emigration to other countries	Freedom of movement is necessary because Kosovo is a small territory and so are the neighboring countries. Economic cooperation benefits each country from free access. Kosovo should enforce more the level of security at home to make sure that transit travels are checked, or who gets in and out.

			Relations with Serbia not yet normalized; there is a risk from clashes between Albanians and Serb as long as enclaves remain and the Serbs feel insecure. The Government of Kosovo must guarantee security for the Serbs.
Political environment	Democratic with new political parties	Unresolved political status with the risk of generating social tensions,	
Economic environment	Liberal and appropriate. Modern legislation in full compliance with the EU standards	Small market; large size of informal sector. Low level of economic development.	Greater political stability is needed to ensure better economic environment.
Population	Young, relatively well-educated and Western oriented.	High unemployment and poverty.	Advantage for economic development; abundance of labor force, but not diversified in skills.
Institutions	New and modern; established with the support of international organizations, including the EU; greater chances to adapt to modern trends.	Still cannot decide on major issues without permission of UNMIK; Lack of experience and maturity in management.	Some aspects of major decision-makings are still retained by UNMIK. They should be all handed over to Kosovo's institutions. UNMIK may exercise the role of policy advisor in the first years of independence, but not beyond.
Internationa l and EU presence	Good opportunities to benefit from their experience and getting ready more quickly for integration.	Incompatibility and lack of adequate coordination between the works of different organizations and envoys.	Some international envoys or personnel of the UN or the EU serve abroad to look also after their personal or group interests. When these interests follow the principle that brings benefits to them at first, the mission may lead to suboptimal results.
Natural resources	Abundance of natural resources, especially minerals.	Lack of investment in their manufacturing and processing capacities. Lack of subsidies to support	Some enterprises are still in social ownership. Their quicker privatization will enable a greater use of these

		and protect agriculture.	resources. Supporting agriculture development is important to lower unemployment in rural areas.
Trade	Liberal trade regime and trade openness	Limited competitiveness at home; heavy reliance on imports and huge trade deficit causing structural distortions.	Has got some good preconditions to lower the deficit in certain products; needs to redefine trade relations with Serbia and control products of other countries coming through Macedonia on fake invoicing basis.
Euro	Strong and stable currency; a step ahead Western Balkan countries towards the EU.	High prices of products and services compared to neighboring countries	Monetary dependence from abroad. Lack of monetary policy. Large quantities of imports make much of the amounts end up abroad.
Physical Infra-structure	Relatively good; easy to access every corner of Kosovo within couple of hours; telecommunication network relatively good.	Frequent power shortages raising costs of doing business.	Infrastructure still needs expanding; current infrastructure needs investment for maintenance; large potentials to generate electricity for itself and export.
Attracting FDI	Good conditions: i) low taxes; ii) appropriate privatization method; iii) natural resources; iv) strong currency in use; v) high purchasing power through remittances and international personnel in Kosovo; vi) cheap labor force.	Risk from informal sector causing unfair competition; higher costs to do business as long as some segments of infrastructure are not improved.	FDI in Kosovo are more likely to evolve alongside trade pattern with developed countries, or FDI may be expected to come from developed countries with which Kosovo carries a great deal of trade.

4.6   Conclusions

Kosovo is still an unusual case of transition awaiting its final political status after more than six years of international administration which has been supporting reconstruction and economic development. An outlook of this six year period of Kosovo's emerging transition and integration in the region and the EU reveals several specifics which can be used as advantages; that Kosovo is an open country, it has a strong currency in use, has got international and European presence supporting its transition which has been delayed for a decade. So far Kosovo has been able to catch in transition processes compared to neighboring countries. Its economy remains dependent on international support, remittances, business at home and imports.

Kosovo's economy suffers from a number of structural distortions which we identified to come primarily from heavy dependence on imports or trade deficit. A number of approaches suggested in this paper are to keep some existing advantages in progress, tackle disadvantages and attempt to gradually diminish disturbing effects of trade deficit. The results may not be immediate but those approaches at least pave the way toward improvements in providing sustainable economic development. To come to that point, it is better to consider an overall strategy of development because many segments are priority. By not prioritizing the challenges identified here, a common priority of all of them probably is a more efficient and responsible management. If resources are managed and used in a better way, that would be an indication of exercising bottom up pressure. With many resources available and good conditions to attract FDI, Kosovo has a chance to make a great leap forward provided a *better use of minds*. The way ahead is to model the strategies that require recognition of Kosovo's unique situation a, including first of all historical and cultural factors, regional issues and modern events.

Like transition, the UN mission in Kosovo is also unique in terms of resources involved and timeframe. It is not known exactly when this mission will be over as some sort of monitoring may be needed in the fist years of Kosovo's independence. Pending political status is a game with unknown results and as long as it lasts, it will be counterproductive. A real challenge here for Kosovo will be to normalize relations with Serbia. National divergences may pose a difficulty to tighter integration not only between Kosovo and Serbia but also in the region. What Western Balkan countries can and should do is the move towards political stability as a gateway of cooperation and other integration processes. The experience from the past has shown that whenever national divergences have a tendency of dominating or subordinating another nation, they become a potential source of destabilization giving rise to inter-ethnic conflicts and make prospects for integration just go right out of the window. That is unlikely to happen as the presence and influence of the EU is there to support stability and to make sure that the past is no longer repeated. One day Kosovo will find itself in the EU, though it is better to move there as a more independent country and release itself a little from 'inferiority complex'.

Bibliography

BARRET, L. (2002): Business in the Balkans: The Case for Cross-Border Co-operation, Center for European Reform, London.

BICANIC, I. (1996): The Economic Divergence of Yugoslavia's Successor States in: Jeffries, I. (ed.), Problems of Economic and Political Transition in the Balkans, Pinter, London, pp. 131-149.

BRADA, J. C., KUTAN, A. M. AND YIGIT, T. M. (2004): The Effects of Transition and Political Instability on Foreign Direct Investment Inflows: Central Europe and the Balkans, Working Paper No. 729, the William Davidson Institute, University of Michigan.

BOS, J. AND VAN DE LAAR, M. (2004): Explaining Foreign Direct Investment in Central and Eastern Europe: An Extended Gravity Approach, Working Paper No. 8, De Nederlandsche Bank, Amsterdam.

BANKING AND PAYMENT AUTHORITY OF KOSOVO (2005): Monthly Statistics Bulletin No. 41, January 2005, Prishtina.

CAMPOS, N. F. AND KINOSHITA, Y. (2003): Why Does FDI Go Where it Goes? New Evidence from the Transition Economies, Working Paper No. 228, IMF, Washington D.C.

CARSTENSEN, K. AND TOUBAL, F. (2004): Foreign Direct Investment in Central and Eastern European Countries: A Dynamic Panel Analysis, Journal of Comparative Economics, Vol. 32, No. 1, pp. 3–22.

CHESAPEAKE ASSOCIATES (2001): Obstacles to Trade, Growth, Investment and Competitiveness: Ten Case Studies on Balkan Business, The Balkan Network Competitiveness Project, Washington D.C.

DAMIJAN, J. P. AND MAJCEN, B. (2001): Trade Reorientation, Firm Performance and Restructuring of Slovenian Manufacturing Sector, Proceedings of the Fourth International Conference on 'Enterprise in Transition, Faculty of Economics, Split, Split-Hvar, May 24-26, 2001, pp. 2478-2492.

COMMISSION OF THE EUROPEAN UNION (2002): The Stabilisation and Association Process for South East Europe, European Commission, First Annual Report, Brussels.

EUROPEAN STABILITY INITIATIVE – ESI (2002): Western Balkans 2004: Assistance, Cohesion and the new Boundaries of Europe – A call for Policy Reform, European Stability Initiative, Berlin – Brussels – Sarajevo.

EUROPEAN COMMISSION (2004): CARDS Assistance Programme to the Western Balkans: Regional Strategy Paper 2002-2006, European Commission, Brussels.

GLENNY, M. (2004): The Kosovo Question and Regional Stability, in Batt, J., The Western Balkans: Moving On, Chaillot Paper No. 70, Institute for Security Studies, Paris, pp. 87-97.

HOLZNER M., GLIGOROV V. (2004): Illegal Trade in South East Europe, paper presented at the IBEU Interim Meeting Functional Borders and Sustainable Security: Integrating the Balkans in the European Union, Athens, May 14-16, 2004.

HUNYA, G. (2004): FDI Policy for Kosovo, Consultant's Report prepared for the Riinvest Institute, Prishtina.

INTERNATIONAL CRISIS GROUP – ICG (2001): Kosovo: a Strategy for Economic Development, ICG Balkans Report No. 123, Brussels.

_____ (2005): Kosovo: Toward Final Status, Europe Report No. 161, Brussels.

INTERNATIONAL MONETARY FUND (2004): Aide Memoire: International Monetary Fund Staff Visit to Kosovo, March 10–19, IMF, Washington D.C.

_____ (2005): Aide Memoire: International Monetary Fund Staff Visit to Kosovo, April 20 – May 4, IMF, Washington D.C.

INDEX KOSOVA (2002): Kosova: The Most Optimistic Country in the World, findings of a public opinion poll with 1,000 Kosovo citizens conducted in Nov. 2001, Prishtina, http://www.indexkosova.com/Publications/Pub_jan02.htm

JUGOSLOVENSKI PREGLED, (1989): The Constitution of the Socialist Federal Republic of Yugoslavia (1974), Jugoslovenska Stvarnost, Beograd.

KEKIC, L. (2004): Foreign Direct Investment in the Balkans: Recent Trends and Prospects, Central and Eastern Europe Economist Intelligence Unit, Athens.

LUCAS, R.E.B. (2005): International Migration to the High-Income Countries: Some Consequences for Economic Development in the Sending Countries, in Bourguignon, F., Pleskovic, B. and Sapir, A., Eds., Are We on Track to Achieve the Millennium Development Goals?, Annual World Bank Conference on Development Economics – Europe 2005, pp. 127-162.

MACK, O. (2003): National Income Accounts: Measurement, Practice, and Welfare Implications of the Initial Estimates of Kosovo's GDP, Contemporary Economic Policy, Vol. 21, No. 2, pp. 186-199.

MICHALOPOULOS, C. (2003): Kosovo's International Trade: Trade Policy, Institutions and Market Access Issues, Report to the UK Department for International Development.

MINISTRY OF ECONOMY AND FINANCE (2005): Kosovo Economy in 2004 and its Prospects for 2005, Ministry of Economy and Finance of the Government of Kosovo, Prishtina, 2005.

MULAJ, I. (2005): Delayed Privatization in Kosovo: Causes, Consequences and Implications in the Ongoing Process, in: Kusic, S., ed., Path-dependent Development in the Western Balkans: The Impact of Privatization, Peter Lang, Frankfurt, pp. 123-163.

MUSTAFA, M., SADIKU, M., MUSTAFA, I., HAVOLLI, Y., AND MULAJ, I. (2001): Prospects for Economic Development in Kosova and Regional Context, prepared for the Vienna Institute of International Economic Studies in terms of the project Long-term Development of South Eastern Europe, www.wiiw.ac.at/balkan/files/Mustafa+.pdf

PINTO, R. (2004): The SME Sector in the Cards Countries: A Panorama at Country and Regional Level, Pohl Consulting & Associates, Prishtina.

RIINVEST (1999): War Consequences on Family Economies and Businesses, Survey Report, Riinvest, Prishtina.

_____ (2001): Key Issues in Building a Taxation Policy in Kosova, Research Report, Riinvest, Prishtina.

_____ (2002): Foreign Direct Investment in Kosova: Policy Environment and Promotional Strategy, Research Report, Riinvest, Prishtina.

_____ (2003): Trade Policies and Export Promotion in Kosova, Research Report, Riinvest, Prishtina.

RILINDJA (1974): Kushtetuta e Krahinës Socialiste Autonome të Kosovës (The Constitution of the Socialist Autonomous Province of Kosova), Rilindja, Prishtina.

SCHNEIDER, F. (2004): The Size of the Shadow Economies of 145 Countries all over the World: First Results over the Period 1999 to 2003, Discussion Paper No. 1431, Institute for the Study of Labor, Bonn.

SLAVESKI, T., AND NEDANOVSKI, P. (2002): Foreign Direct Investment in the Balkans, Eastern European Economics, Vol. 40, No. 4, pp. 83-99.

STATISTICAL OFFICE OF KOSOVO (2004): Kosovo in Figures 2004, Statistical Office of Kosovo, Prishtina.

_____ (2002): A Household Budget Survey 2002/2003, Statistical Office of Kosovo, Prishtina

THE ECONOMIST (1993): 363 Quadrillion Per Cent Inflation, Vol. 329, No. 7832, p.60, 10/9/1993, London.

UNMIK (2004): Trade Policy for Kosovo, a Joint Paper by Ministry of Trade and Industry and UNMIK European Union Pillar, Prishtina.

UVALIC, M. (2005): Trade Liberalisation in Southeast Europe: Recent Trends and Some Policy Implications, UNECE Spring Seminar on Financing for Development in the ECE Region: Promoting Growth in Low-income Transition Economies, Geneva (21 February).

WORLD BANK (2000): Economic Reform for Peace and Reconciliation: Kosovo, Federal Republic of Yugoslavia, Volume I, II, the World Bank, Washington D.C. (June 30).

WORLD BANK (2003): Trade Policies and Institutions in the Countries of South Eastern Europe in the EU Stabilization and Association Process, Washington, D.C.

_____ (2004): Kosovo: Economic Memorandum, Report No: 28023-KOS, Washington, D.C.

_____ (2005): Kosovo Poverty Assessment: Promoting Opportunity, Security, and Participation for All, Report No. 32378-XK (June), Poverty Reduction and Economic Management Unit of the World Bank, Washington D.C.

Chapter 5

Siniša Kušić and Claudia Grupe:

Scrutinising EU Policy: Does Intra-Regional Cooperation in the Western Balkans Contribute to Economic Progress?

5.1 Abstract

The main motivation for regional cooperation in the Western Balkans is provided by the EU, formulating it as conditional for the countries' EU accession aspirations. Economically, this claim includes the establishment of regional free trade agreements (RTAs) whose direct economic effects are twofold and limited: Whereas inflows of FDI are likely to increase due to a bigger market, an increase of interregional trade will be moderate and might even stall microeconomic restructuring.

To gain considerable profits from regional economic integration, transnational linkages on a microeconomic level as the emergence of cross-border alliances, joint efforts to conquer West European markets, or cooperation in R&D to enhance innovation are needed. Gains from a RTA thus will be of indirect nature: Long term profits result only from overcoming the aversions against regional partnerships and from the re-emergence of mutual trust.

5.2 Introduction

The European Union (EU) leaves no doubt that it expects the countries in South Eastern Europe to move together closer and to show their preparedness for regional cooperation. After the status of the region had been undefined for a longer time (Uvalić, 2000), the EU developed an instrument to establish peace in the region, and to set the appropriate conditions for an accelerating catching-up through the Stabilisation and Association process (SAp), targeting the six countries of the Western Balkans.[50]

The cornerstone of the SAp is set by the Stabilisation and Association Agreements (SAA). The conclusion of the SAA represents the signatories' commitment to complete over a transition period a formal association with the EU. As stabilisation and development are considered to be operatively determined by the intensification of regional integration, the implementation of the SAA is based on the gradual implementation of a free trade area and reforms designed to achieve the adoption of EU standards with the aim of moving closer to the EU. Regional cooperation, including the other South East European countries, has been formulated as a precondition for an EU accession of the countries in the Western Balkans.

Apart from establishing political and economic conditionality for the development of bilateral relations between the EU and the Western Balkans, the SAp includes economic and financial assistance, budgetary assistance and balance of payment support, assistance for democratisation and civil society, humanitarian aid for refugees, returnees and other persons of concern, cooperation in justice and home affairs, and the development of a political dialogue.

Whereas the EU's instrument broadly refers to the creation of multiple ties and interactions linking people or institutions across the borders of the distinct states, the paper will take a narrower view and concentrate on the economic effects of the EU's approach, so that the effects of a free trade area (FTA) in South Eastern Europe will be analysed. However, although taking

---

[50] In accordance with the notation of the EU, the term Western Balkans in this paper will refer to Albania (AL), Bosnia and Hercegovina (BiH), Croatia (HR), Macedonia (MK), and Serbia and Montenegro. As there are in most cases only aggregated figures for the only recently divided country of Serbia and Montenegro, this paper will treat the two countries as one and refer to it as SCG. South East European (SEE) countries are the Western Balkans plus Bulgaria (BG), Moldova (MD), and Romania (RO).

economic analysis into focus and as a starting point, it will not be neglected that the process is in fact taking part on different levels of society - politically, socially, legally, historically, culturally etc. - that are reinforcing one another.

The paper will analyse the role of regional integration and the by this means facilitated cooperation in the Western Balkans and its effects on economic performance and interactions with the medium- to long-term perspective of an EU-accession. It will be assessed whether regional integration can foster economic growth of the small economies and in how far overcoming the under-developed markets and the creation of an integrated South East European market with improved labour division will attract additional foreign capital and stimulate trade. The economic analysis of the effects of a free trade area will be the fundament of discussion. Starting with a short overview on the theory of regional economic integration, its theoretical predictions will be applied to the special case of integration in the Western Balkans. Based on these evaluations, the paper finishes with a discussion of measures that could be taken to convert the regional cooperation that is often merely cheap talk into real economic outcomes.

5.3   The Effects of Regional Integration

5.3.1   The Theory of Regional Integration

Regional integration is the institutional unification of independent national economies to bigger economic entities. The term must be distinguished from regional cooperation which involves cooperative or collaborative efforts, common interests, or common issues that do not stop at the country border. In the terminology of the paper, regional integration will directly refer to the creation of a South East European free trade area, whereas cooperation as the broader concept denotes any form of joint efforts. Regional cooperation will often be facilitated by the creation of an economically integrated area, so that the success of regional cooperative efforts is to some degree dependent on the institutionalised unification in terms of integration.

Research on regional integration has mainly considered the conditions for an efficient use of resources on a regional basis. This includes the elimination of all barriers on mobility of goods and factors, but also the creation of efficient markets and institutions supporting the integration. Integration requires a reduction of national sovereignty, nevertheless, states submit to these restrictions in their political powers. Reasons are both political and economic aspects favouring regional integration (Robson, 1998). According to the classical and neoclassical trade theory respectively, whose most famous approach is the Heckscher-Ohlin-Theorem, countries are equipped with different production factors that are used by trade in the form of comparative advantages. In the context of international labour division, economies thus specialise on those products which can be created under comparative cost advantages. Through free trade, the factor costs for labour and capital adjust and the resources of different countries complement each other (Viner, 1950; Robson, 1998). Returns to scale are constant, markets are perfect and complete, and transport costs do not exist. If polypolistic structures are paired with equal rates of investment and equal access to technological knowledge, the growth of an economy is only determined through population growth and technological progress. According to the neoclassic convergence hypothesis, relatively underdeveloped countries will then catch-up to higher developed countries. However, absolute convergence will only appear if the structural conditions of two countries are similar (Krugman and Obstfeld, 2003).

The traditional model according to Viner however suffers from important shortcomings, which have been taken into account and ruled out by the new trade theory that shows that profits can emerge independently of the existence of comparative advantages (Venables, 1987): For the neoclassic assumption to hold, the integration partners' trade structure is necessarily asymmetric. This assumption and the assumption of polypolistic markets are hurt in reality: The prevalence of intra-industry trade, i.e. trade in similar products, is difficult to explain in terms of comparative advantages, and product differentiation seems to be the driving force behind this kind of trade. This implies imperfect competition as each producer has market power in its own varieties. Competition is less likely to be based on prices than on innovation, as profits are generated from offering a differentiated bundle of goods. This specialisation enforced by trade tends to intensify (Krugman and Obstfeld, 2003).

The increasing importance of multinational corporations is another indication that imperfect competition matters, since a key explanation for the existence of such firms is that they have firm-specific advantages to bring to their hosts.

A third basic constraint on the validity of classical and neo-classical theories is the assumption of constant returns to scale and perfect competition (Walz, 1999). On a long term, however, dynamic more than static effects of factor allocation are inducing restructuring and growth. In reality, relative factor endowments and comparative advantages are not given, but in a state of permanent change. Moreover, they not only determine but are also over time determined by the pattern of international trade. Technology-intensive industries give strong incentives for innovation and opportunities for accumulation of physical and human capital, whereas an economy based on primary commodity production gives fewer possibilities for development.

These corrections of the neoclassic theory are necessary with regard to integration processes including less developed economies. In the aftermath of Viner (1950), the theoretic literature on integration focused almost exclusively on industrialised countries. Only starting in the 60s, the question was asked whether the traditional theory of integration was applicable to emerging markets (Balassa, 1965). Especially concerning the relevance of static versus dynamic effects of integration and the weight of economic compared to political purposes, the validity of the neoclassic theory was questioned.

Taking the traditional analysis as a basis, i.e. the ideas of trade creation and trade diversion (Viner, 1950), North-South and South-South regional trade agreements operate in quite different ways. Trade creation increases the specialisation in production and thus welfare, whereas trade-diversion reduces welfare because it shifts production away from comparative advantage. Several studies showed that South-South integration is likely to create trade diversion. Early experiments of South-South integration in Africa and Latin America demonstrated a welfare reduction for the poorest members, trade diversion prevailing over trade creation in most cases. South-South integration tends to lead to divergence of member country incomes. In particular, countries with the highest comparative disadvantage within the area would suffer a welfare reduction (Venables, 2000). On the contrary, if the integration area includes relatively high income countries, it is the lower income country that experiences a welfare gain from trade creation. North-South integration, in contrast, would cause convergence, this creating an incentive for developing countries to establish trade links with industrial countries. Relying on an analysis in terms of trade creation versus trade diversion, North-South are better than South-South arrangements from the point of view of the participating Southern countries (World Bank, 2000).

However, South-South integration - on the theoretical basis of the new trade theory - can provide dynamic welfare effects including enhancing efficiency through mutual learning, increased competition between peers in development, enabling economies of scale and scope, increased attractiveness to FDI, and securing greater bargaining power.

Foremost among the assumed dynamic economic benefits of integration has been the "training ground" effect. For many less developed countries, and particularly for those with very small domestic markets, regional economic integration may offer a valuable experience, facilitating the transition to a more balanced development and a more open economy (Robson, 1998). Within a regional setting, both quality and marketing techniques can improve and promote diversification and export production at a later stage. Integration will benefit customers in the integrated market as well as enhance export production.

However, the training-ground argument has the basic rationale behind infant industry protection and traditional import-substituting development strategies. Arguments in favour of import substitution view existing trade patterns as a source of dominance and exploitation. Extensive government intervention in the economy and protection in the form of tariffs and quotas are considered necessary to break out of the current world division of labour. One of the major problems with import substitution strategies is that the market size of a single country limits the degree of specialisation. Another problem are the distortions created by tariffs and other government interventions in the economy. Protection reduces the incentives to undertake quality and productivity improvements.

A second important argument for South-South integration is that the host country market size is one of the strongest determinants of where foreign firms invest. By reducing the trade barriers within a region, prospective investors can be offered a larger market, in combination with a harmonised investment climate and increased political and macroeconomic stability resulting from a successful integration process, this makes investments more profitable.[51]

Compared to North-South trade, it may thirdly be assumed that the goods of Southern countries are often suited to the needs of other countries on a similar level of development. Furthermore, in theory, commodity prices might be stabilised on a higher level through co-operation. Technology, infrastructure and information, i.e. the joint production of public goods, are also considered promising fields for co-operation. Although this is in most instances a matter of co-operation, possible without integration, a close relationship between integrated economies can make it easier for politicians to reach agreements, especially as one serious obstacle to South-South trade are transportation problems resulting from insufficient infrastructure. Also, corruption as a devastating problem in many emerging markets can be more easily fought in a system of harmonised regulation (Shleifer and Vishny, 1993). Finally, shared marketing and distribution may in some industries make it possible to bring the commodities closer to the final customers, thereby increasing profit.

Finally, in addition to the improved access to large Northern markets and improved supply of intermediate goods due to lower tariffs, regional integration arrangements can speed up the adoption of new technologies by the least developed regions. Furthermore, it may give these members access to more advanced institutions and policy instruments. Although this may take place within South-South integration schemes, the potential for technology

---

[51] The experience of Mexico within NAFTA, and of Portugal and Spain within the EC, back this argument that integration can have a positive effect on investments (Baldwin and Venables, 1995).

transfer is much bigger within integration schemes involving both developing and developed countries.

As a conclusion, it may be stated that the simultaneity of North-South and South-South integration appears as the most-promising strategy. Developing country participation in North South and South South arrangements makes it possible for integration to occur in various directions - within and between countries of both South and North.

5.3.2 Background and Economic Performance of the Western Balkans

Unlike in central Europe, where regional integration was a consequence rather than a precondition for EU integration, for the Balkans, for political and economic reasons, i.e. their tendency to national insularity and political instability, regional integration is a must.

Croatia as the first country of the Western Balkans opened accession negotiations with the EU, after it had been awarded candidate status on June, 18th when the European Council agreed that Croatia met the political criteria: "The achievement of candidate status by Croatia should be an encouragement to the other countries of the Western Balkans to pursue their reforms", the EU leaders stated, repeating their affirmation that "the future of the Western Balkans rests within the European Union". Equally, the candidate status of Macedonia has underlined this target, yet there is a long way to go: Bridging the transitional period until this credible and concrete scenario becomes reality requires the political will and commitment of the regional leaders that will determine the success of both EU measures - the bilateral association process and regional integration. Since 1990, the region has been economically and politically disintegrated, although the common history, geography, and stage of development would be conducive to regional coordination, cooperation and economic integration. Thus, the conditionality imposed on the region would appear as a force to re-merge formerly integrated countries.

This only partly applies to the region as a whole since Albania had had a quite singular position among all East European transition economies. Even under the era of socialism it turned away from both economic blocks in East and West and followed a policy that was exclusively oriented on autarky and thus was not integrated into the division of labour within COMECON. Today, technology transfer via FDI is relatively low, with regard to the level of education and the potential to create a national innovation system, it is far behind other East and even South East European countries (Horn and Kušić, 2001). By far the most important trading partner is the EU, within it especially Italy and Greece, representing about 75 per cent of Albania's total imports and 90 per cent of its exports (European Economy. European Commission, Directorate-General for Economic and Financial Affairs, 2004).

The other four states, however, share the common heritage of SFR Yugoslavia, that economically and politically was quite a unique state under socialism as well.[52] A look at the data of inter-republic trade in SFRJ would thus imply that the re-integration of the region should be considered a step back to normality. Although there had been a rising regional autarky and fragmentation since the passing of the new constitution in 1974, the inter-republican trade always represented an important part of overall trade in the republics of SFRJ (Uvalić, 2000). The deepening fragmentation manifested itself in increasing domestic sales, the duplication of plants, barriers to the mobility of capital and labour and weak integration of enterprises, but in fact, the interdependence remained stronger than suggested on a political basis. Thus, in 1987, exports to the markets of other republics represented between 13.4 (Serbia including the provinces Vojvodina and Kosovo) and 25 per cent (Montenegro) of total gross material product (Uvalić, 1993).

---

[52] The cornerstones of these uniqueness were: 1. the relative independence of the Soviet Union since 1948, when Josip Broz broke with Stalin, 2. the slow approach to the West since then and 3. the special economic system of workers' self-management. The original self-management concept redesignated enterprises as work organisations of associated labour and divided them into smaller units at the level of factory departments (see e.g. Roggemann (1970) and Stein1980 for details) and since the 1950s and the foreign policy of nonalignment (app. 1956).

Yet with the breakdown of the common market and as a consequence of the war, old trade patterns, distribution structures, existing networks and infrastructure were severely damaged or destroyed, hindering the re-emergence of close economic collaboration although the common history of the four states would strongly suggest increased cooperation on all economic levels.

How heavily the ethnical conflicts impacted not only on political, but also on economic stability, can be shown by a look at the Yugoslav successor state Slovenia, that – ethnically homogenous - survived the breakdown and the war quite unaffectedly. At the end of the 1980s, SFR Yugoslavia had more favouring starting conditions than many other transition countries, resulting from early reforms towards de-centralisation and orientation towards the Western markets, however, the breakdown of common market and state and the armed conflicts destroyed these advantages (Kušić, 2002).

In the last years, commonalities are mainly composed through economic backwardness relative to other transition countries and instability. Intra-regional trade declined significantly, and although one part of this decline could be compensated through unofficial and unregistered trade (smuggling, corruption), this will not contribute to the strengthening of regional integration. Moreover, factors that are conducive to regional integration would be geography and physical proximity, the common heritage of socialism, culture, partly language and social and economic cohesiveness, commonalities that have been partly offset by the experiences in the 1990s. Also economically, despite the relative backwardness, the region is far from being a homogeneous unit, which is also reflected in the main macroeconomic indicators that are presented for the whole South East European region in table 5.1.

Table 5.1: Macroeconomic Indicators (2005)

	Real GDP growth	Consumer prices	Unemployment	Governmental Balance (% of GDP)	Current Account (% of GDP)	External Debt (% of GDP)
AL	5.5	2.4	14.5	-3.3	-7.5	21.4
BiH	5.0	-0.4a 2.4b	40.6c	-1.1	-23.3	34.0
BG	5.5	5.0	11.5	3.2	-11.8	67.7
HR	4.3	3.3	18.0	-4.2	-6.3	82.4
MK	3.8	0.5	36.5	-1.0	-4.4	39.3
MDc	6.3	15.8	7.4	0.2	-8.0	89.2
RO	4.1	9.0	5.8	-0.8	-8.7	38.5
SCG	6.1	15.2	32.5	0.9	-8.7	61.6
CEB[53],c	3.6	3.2	12.0	-3.3	-5.7	54.3
CIS[54],c	7.6	9.1	4.7	-1.2	-2.0	52.7

a: Yearly average in the Federation BiH

b: Yearly average in the Republika Srpska

c: Data for 2003; Source: Sanfey, Falcetti, Taci, and Tepić (2004), p. 6.

Source: Banc Austria Creditanstalt, CEE Report 2-2006

Croatia is at the upper end of the spectrum, its economy in fact accounts for roughly half of the GDP of the Western Balkans. The other six countries in South Eastern Europe are bunched together more closely. Inflation is broadly under control. Overall growth has been higher than in central Europe and the Baltics within the last years. Yet it would take many years with these growth differentials to catch up. Unemployment remains a persistent problem in the region. Croatia has the highest consolidated general government benefit. Trade and current account deficits are typically high for the region.

The main economic incentives for regional cooperation are trade, the regional dimension of problems, investment, and EU integration (Uvalić,

[53] Central Europe and the Baltics

[54] Commonwealth of Independent States

2000). In fact, the common membership in international organisations or - in the case of the Western Balkans – the common goal to join them, the external pressures resulting hereof, and the need to create a stable and peaceful environment create the biggest incentive for cooperation behaviour. The main motivation for intra-regional cooperation is provided by the EU within the setup of compatible free trade arrangements. Whether the claim for their foundation can be justified based on an economic rationale, or whether it is just a means to create political stability will be assessed in the following paragraphs.

5.3.3 Potential Effects of a South East European FTA

Besides ethnical conflicts, the region lacks economic cohesion that is mirrored in the trade patterns and in an insufficient common economic direction of the regional economies. Political inadequacies as flawed democratisation, nationalism, highly centralised or also weak states may be interpreted as barriers to increased cooperation and the set up of free trade arrangements (Anastasakis and Bojicić-Dželilović, 2002). Partly, there are strong resentments against the EU's instrument that is used for the first time and exclusively for the Western Balkans. The hurting consequences of the war do not only weigh heavily on the political relations but tend to have social and psychological effects that partly offset the argument that the countries of the Western Balkans except for Albania have formed a homogenous economic area for decades and thus exhibit potential for increased trade.

Despite the quite significant regional differences on an economic level that are even revealed by a first look at the basic macroeconomic figures in table 5.1 and also reflected in the different stages of agreements with the EU, the integration in South Eastern Europe constitutes a case of South-South integration, whereas the bilateral agreements with the EU constitute a case of North-South integration. Thus, the direct gains from a South East European free trade area appear highly questionable, and will be examined below.

5.3.3.1 Trade patterns in the Western Balkans from a Neoclassic Perspective

The establishment of a South East European free trade area is well in progress. Except for Moldova, all countries have completed negotiations of bilateral free trade agreements (OECD, 2003). The Memorandum of Understanding on Trade Liberalisation and Facilitation was signed in 2001 by Albania, Bosnia and Hercegovina, Bulgaria, Croatia, Macedonia, Romania, and Serbia and Montenegro, then Federal Republic of Yugoslavia (OECD, 2002). In addition to the intra-regional bilateral free trade agreements,[55] all countries of the Western Balkans have preferential free trade agreements with the EU.

The Balkans have been benefiting from duty free access to the EU market for almost all goods, only limited by particular conditions for textile and agricultural products, via a set of autonomous trade measures unilaterally granted by the EU. The Stabilisation and Association Agreements (SAA) that have been signed between the EU and the FYR Macedonia and Croatia respectively furthermore provide the economies with progressive reciprocal free trade of goods. Negotiations with Albania to sign the SAA have started in 2003 and are under negotiation with Bosnia and Hercegovina and Serbia and Montenegro (von Hagen and Traistaru, 2003).

The extent to which the countries under consideration rely on regional trade and on trade with the EU respectively is presented in table 5.2. The intensity index, calculated both for the EU-25 and the SEE-7[56], indicates that these countries tend to trade with the specified regions more than those regions' weight in world trade would suggest (indicator is larger than unity). A potential reason may be the geographical proximity of the markets, yet the intensity

---

[55] For an overview see European Economy. European Commission, Directorate-General for Economic and Financial Affairs (2004).

[56] As – despite of the newly changed status of Montenegro to an independent state – we treat Serbia and Montenegro as one country due to the unavailability of disaggregated data, we name Albania, Bosnia and Hercegovina, Bulgaria, Croatia, Macedonia, Romania, Serbia and Montenegro still the SEE-7, in accordance with availability of data and earlier notation.

index within the region is extremely high and takes most often values in two digits. This indicates an over reliance on intraregional trade and underlines the need for greater market diversification concerning exports.

Yet it should be annotated that whereas the region seems to be an important export destination for all countries except Albania, it is a very modest source of imports, except for Bosnia and Hercegovina, although the overall trading of the country has been declining in the last years. Albania is the regionally least integrated country, and there have been no trends that this would change, on the contrary, the intensity of trade within the region is further declining. In all countries over 50 per cent of the exports are destined to the EU, which is also the largest source of imports. Therefore, apart from Croatia, there is a continuous decline in the intensity indices associated with the SEE region, with a rise in exports to the EU-25.

Also looking at the propensity to trade with the region, taking into consideration that the countries may have opened up so much that despite of declining intensities there might still have been a rising propensity to trade with the region, we see that in Albania, Bulgaria, Serbia and Montenegro, and Macedonia the propensity indices tended to decline in trade with the SEE-7; whereas in Bosnia and Hercegovina and in Romania the propensity to trade with both regions increased. Only Croatia shows a declining propensity to trade with the EU and an increasing interest in the SEE region.

Table 5.2: Coefficients of the Intensity and Propensity to Trade of SEE

	EU-25			SEE-7		
	1996	2000	2004	1996	2000	2004
Intensity [a] of trade with the region						
Albania	2.19	2.44	2.23	9.19	7.74	2.51
Bosnia and Herzegovina	1.15	1.25	1.33	59.98	55.86	48.49
Bulgaria	1.04	1.42	1.44	20.95	27.50	13.88
Croatia	1.74	1.82	1.59	30.53	34.73	31.32
Romania	1.52	1.83	1.80	8.21	12.84	8.39
Serbia and Montenegro	0.96	1.26	1.31	75.83	61.52	45.87
The former Yugoslav Republic						
of Macedonia	1.28	1.23	1.41	57.51	64.05	39.76
Turkey	1.32	1.45	1.36	4.86	5.82	5.43
Propensity [b] to trade with the region						
Albania	0.15	0.17	0.18	0.64	0.55	0.20
Bosnia and Herzegovina	0.02	0.30	0.26	1.27	13.39	9.43
Bulgaria	0.52	0.54	0.59	10.35	10.53	5.71
Croatia	0.39	0.44	0.37	6.93	8.35	7.32
Romania	0.34	0.51	0.58	1.87	3.59	2.69
Serbia and Montenegro	0.11	0.30	0.21	8.72	14.63	7.42
The former Yugoslav Republic						
of Macedonia	0.33	0.45	0.44	14.87	23.55	12.42
Turkey	0.17	0.20	0.29	0.62	0.81	1.14

[a] *"Intensity of trade with a given region" is determined as follows: Iij = (xij /xi)/(mj/mw-i), where xij is country i's exports going to the region j, xi is country i's total exports, mj is total imports of the region j and mw-i is world imports (net of country i's imports). An index larger than unity means that country i trades with region j more than j's weight in world trade.*

[b] *"Propensity to export to a given region" is determined as follows: Pij = (xij /GDPi)/(mj/mw-i).*

Source: Gaučaitė Wittich (2005), p. 6.

Given that the absolute level of intra-regional trade is low, especially concerning the level of imports, and that the interest in it is even further declining, as the table shown above presents, some authors argue that the countries can in fact not be considered to form a region in economic terms (Gligorov, 1998; Christie, 2002). The breakdown of the common market at the beginning of the 1990s terminated traditional trade links. Today, there is a revival of trade between Croatia and the Federation Bosnia and Hercegovina and between Serbia and the Republika Srpska.

Yet it should be noted that a high proportion of trade is likely not to be included in the statistics as it takes unofficial forms. A part of trade is thus illegal or takes the form of barter that is not reflected in the statistics. The data therefore probably underestimate the true level of intra-regional trade in the Western Balkans.

Nevertheless, there are good reasons to assume that although there are still some non-tariff trade barriers in South Eastern Europe, the main reason that keeps actual and potential trade rather low is related to similar trade structures and little complementarities. Experiences with CEFTA and existing trade and specialisation patterns suggest low level of potential intra-regional trade, especially given the small size of the regional market and similar competitive advantages (Vlahinić-Dizdarević and Kušić, 2004). To a large extend, the comparative advantages are therefore overlapping, as table 5.3 presents, showing the revealed comparative advantages of the region in 2002.[57]

---

[57] The theoretical foundation of the RCA is the Heckscher-Ohlin theorem according to which countries have comparative advantages in trading with goods with which it is sufficiently endowed. See Balassa (1989), p. 43.

Table 5.3: Comparative Advantages (2002)

	Primary commodities		Labour-intensive and resource-based manufactures		Low skill and technology intensity		Medium skill and technology intensity		High skill and technology intensity	
	Average 1996-1998	Average 2002-2004	Average 1996-1998	Average 2002-2004	Average 1996-1998	Average 2002-2004	Average 1996-1998	Average 2002-2004	Average 1996-1998	Average 2002-2004
Albania	-1.3	-31.6	87.1	138.4	-4.1	-4.3	-52.1	-61.9	-29.6	-40.6
Bosnia and Herzegovina	..	57.1	..	21.8		-0.2		-25.2		-53.5
Bulgaria	41.9	58.5	-3.0	58.6	36.4	23.7	-52.4	-88.4	-22.8	-52.4
Croatia	18.2	26.2	63.0	41.7	16.5	24.8	-75.4	-64.0	-22.3	-28.7
Romania	0.5	-1.3	88.2	89.9	50.9	18.0	-70.5	-44.3	-69.1	-62.2
Serbia and Montenegro[b]	56.6	93.3	-7.2	20.2	26.3	9.9	-19.3	-43.9	-56.3	-79.4
The former Yugoslav Republic of Macedonia	7.6	-11.1	78.2	132.5	48.9	51.7	-68.1	-83.2	-66.7	-89.9
Turkey	21.0	-12.6	161.1	135.4	6.0	22.3	-127.5	-44.8	-60.6	-100.3
SEE-7[c]	19.5	19.2	54.4	74.9	36.1	19.1	-63.4	-57.2	-46.6	-56.0
SEE-8[c]	20.5	1.4	115.6	106.1	19.0	20.6	-101.0	-49.1	-54.1	-79.0
Memorandum item:										
New EU-8	9.4	-0.4	41.5	24.2	17.8	4.0	-21.2	11.6	-47.5	-39.4

RCA is measured by the CTB indicator.

CTB = [(xik-mik)/(xi+mi)-((xi-mi)/(xi+mi))*((xik+mik)/(xi+mi))]*10,000, where i denotes country, k denotes commodity, x stands for exports and m for imports. CTB compares country i's actual trade balance for a given commodity to the "expected" (or "neutral") balance, assuming that each commodity contributes to total trade in proportion to its weight. A positive contribution is interpreted as a "revealed comparative advantage" for trade in that commodity, and a negative, as a "revealed comparative disadvantage". By definition, the sum of CTBs for all commodities is zero.

[b] Data for Serbia and Montenegro refer to 2002 instead of the average for 2002-2004.

[c] Aggregates for 1996-1998 exclude Bosnia and Hercegovina.

Source: Gaučaitė Wittich (2005), p. 14.

The calculation of the indicator shows that there is a dominance of raw materials and labour-intensive products, pointing to little potential to develop sustainable competitiveness. The analysis indicates that the economies compete on the same external markets. Given the low elasticities of demand on these markets, implying low growth potential, development strategies should better focus on the upgrading of production structures and differentiated products (Kušić and Grupe, 2004).

In fact, labour-intensive products make up the largest part of exports for all countries. The trade structure reflects inter-industry specialisation patterns typical for developing countries in their exchanges with developing countries, as capital intensive products account for more than one-third of imports (von Hagen and Traistaru, 2003).

At the present stage, the Western Balkans compete on the basis of low costs in similar branches, the extend to which intra-regional trade may unfold is thus limited. Actually, empirical studies back this assumption. Christie (2002) was able to show a highly distorted pattern in terms of bilateral distribution of trade flows for the waning 1990s. Using a gravity approach, here - estimated the trade potentials for the SEE-7 for 1999 without using any dummy variables affecting South Eastern Europe.[58] The actual level of trade between Serbia and Montenegro and Croatia is then close to the base estimate, whereas trade between Bosnia and Hercegovina and both Croatia and Serbia and Montenegro is high above the estimate.

Integrating estimates with potential GDP and dummies for EU membership and regional integration (i.e. inclusion of a CEFTA dummy), there is scope for strongly increased trade between Croatia and Serbia and Montenegro. In contrast, even then the level of Bosnian imports in 1999 was in fact far higher than the estimate. Also, the trade of Serbia and Montenegro with Macedonia in 1999 was far above the calculated potential in all model specifications. However, it has to be taken into account that trade sanctions and the NATO's military intervention in 1999 strongly directed Serbia's trade towards selected neighbours and Russia, so that there is a large scope for significant redirection. In fact, Macedonia's trade is high above potential with all regional countries.

To conclude, Christie (2002) found that there was a strong overtrade between Bosnia and Hercegovina and both Croatia and Serbia, whereas the trade flow between Croatia and Serbia could increase dramatically in case of

---

[58] Dummies specific to South Eastern Europe can be considered to correct for abnormal situations. Leaving out these corrections enables a comparison of potential flows with current flows. Christie (2002), p. 12.

common integration. From the point of view of trade, SEE could not be considered a region due to very low trade flows given the geographic proximity; moreover, he expected the countries to elaborate their trade links with the EU.

The results have been confirmed by Kaminski and de la Rocha (2003) who calculated a gravity model for 2000. Again, trade between Serbia and Montenegro and Croatia stays 80 per cent below its potential. The overtrade between Croatia and Bosnia and Hercegovina of about 56 per cent is explained by the special relations between Croatia and the Federation, whereas distinct linkages between the Republika Srpska and Serbia and Montenegro also explain as the overtrade which exceeds the predicted level by 29 per cent.

Thus, except for bilateral trade between Croatia and Serbia and Montenegro there is not much room for increasing trade flows within the successor states of former SFRJ. The calculation of the gravity model changed dramatically when Albania was included, indicating that the potential for growth is 70 per cent. However, due to the autarchic policy Albania followed under socialism, there are still no transportation facilities or commercial linkages with the rest of the Western Balkans so that an expansion as big as predicted is unlikely to occur as long as there is no adequate infrastructure (Kaminski and de la Rocha, 2003).

To conclude, on the basis of these estimates of the effects of a FTA on trade in the region, thus the direct effects of the FTA, the economic justification of the EU's instrument appears porous. The rise in exports and imports since the 1990s was accompanied by gains in the relative importance of EU partners. The growing dependence on the EU, particularly the increasingly heavy reliance on outsourcing orders from EU firms seems to have resulted in a narrowing of the commodity mix of SEE exports.

In addition, it has to be noted that the markets of the Western Balkans are rather small and thus the stimulus for further trade is smaller than that provided by the accession to the EU (Anastasakis and Bojicić-Dželilović, 2002). However, there might be indirect effects of the FTA to the degree that the increasing cooperation creates stability, thus attracts investors and makes room for cross-border alliances.

5.3.3.2 Potential Effects of a South East European FTA from the Perspective of the New Trade Theory

As the scale for intra-regional trade is limited, the focus of trade policies is on the markets of the EU. However, to benefit from the process of intra-regional integration and to stand the competitive pressures originating in the EU, the economies of the Western Balkans need to develop competitive production structures. Further reliance on low factor costs will not bring the desired catching up; instead to proceed, the enterprises of the distinct countries need to develop differentiated products, that find customers both in the increasing South East European market and in the single market of the EU and move up the skills and technology to sustain rising wages and permit greater economies of scale and scope in production (UNCTAD, 2002).

Whereas an application of the neoclassic trade theory has yielded the result that the scope of the effects through creation of a free trade area would be limited, we will now put the hypothesis of the new trade theory against the specific situation of the Western Balkans and access the extent to which effects of intra-regional integration as put forward by the new trade theory can help achieving the aim of increasing competitiveness.

5.3.3.2.1 The Training Ground Effect

In the context of South-South integration, it is often argued and hoped for that this form of integration was more viable and effective than others devised to help developing countries enter the global economy, offering a useful training ground for countries to educate and prepare themselves before taking on more complex global economic endeavours. Governance, capacity-building, health, education, environment, science and technology, and trade and investment are fields often regarded as especially conducive for regional integration.

However, what makes a country competitive and thus successful on international markets are basically its enterprises. The mere institutional framework needs to provide the necessary general conditions (Kušić and Grupe, 2004).

The orientation towards regional and often familiar markets where the patterns of demand are less sophisticated appears yet unlikely to help overcome the lacking competitiveness. On the one hand, it can be assumed that the re-orientation towards local customers is a means of evading the competitive pressure in Western Europe and thus of delaying necessary steps of modernisation and restructuring.[59] The strong promotion of a FTA may thus even stall microeconomic restructuring. This is one reason that underlines the necessity of a simultaneous approach to the EU.

On the other hand, turning to regional markets may help preparing for increasingly competitive situations if it includes the establishment of networks and alliances. Due to the common heritage, local brands can be more easily distributed and sold than to markets of the EU, but probably also more easily than products coming from the West. In this respect, the regional setting may be a training ground, but only if this process is accompanied by a upgrading of general management skills that cover all aspects of marketing, distribution, after-sales service and continuous upgrading and innovation management.

Deficiencies in these areas are prevalent in enterprises of each country of the region, and setting a coherent and consistent framework may help to reduce them. Enterprises suffer from insufficient information regarding the legal framework, taxation, finance, and standards. Further difficulties are imposed on them by restrictive employment legislation and social barriers (Bartlett and Bukvič, 2002). In addition, many enterprises in the region suffer from liquidity problems and high liabilities, so that their capability for regional integration is a priori limited (Altmann, 2002). A harmonisation of certain conditions would help them find their way to regional domestic markets and thus strengthen themselves for the competition with the West. At present,

---

[59] See Grupe and Kušić (2004) for a study on high-technology enterprises in Croatia that backs the assumption that the main problem in entering the EU was branding of domestic products. This is why most enterprises tended to orient themselves to regional markets, were the costs of adoption and of setting up sales channels are perceived to be significantly lower.

market entry barriers, most notably in forms of inadequate mobility of capital and labour, exist and do thus not contribute to mutual interaction and support. For that purpose, formalities and procedures need to be simplified, laws and regulations must be harmonised, infrastructure be improved.

5.3.3.2.2 Economies of Scale and the Attraction of FDI

An economy's present and prospective trade flows are positively correlated with the size of its market. Markets in the Western Balkans, as a consequence of political disintegration, became increasingly smaller and less efficient during the last years, and were protected through newly created trade barriers. Decreasing incomes, record level unemployment, and worse standards of living in turn let decline the purchasing power of the region.

Economies of scale in the Western Balkans can only be achieved when the small states create a market of 25 million people that benefits producers and investors and erases all barriers to free movement of persons, goods, and capital.

Especially the capacity to attract foreign direct investment (FDI) is a crucial aspect of growth for the Western Balkans. FDI are not only an important source of financing of large trade and current account deficits, but are recognised as a source of positive spillover effects, ranging from the transfer of technology and know how to increased local competition and the creation of employment opportunities, and the provision of access to international markets for foreign producers (Dunning, 1993).

At a microeconomic level, direct technology transfer, contagion and knowledge diffusion improve productivity and efficiency in local firms (Blomstrom and Kokko, 1997). Local suppliers, in addition, benefit from foreign investors' management skills and are forced to meet higher standards of quality, so that FDI enhance competition.

In the 1990s, the Balkans have gone through a series of security shocks inducing large political and economic shocks that were enforced by prevalent nationalism, creating a region that was averting investments rather than attracting them. FDI that are mainly of a market-seeking nature, will only flow to the Western Balkans if the market is sufficiently huge (Dunning, 1993). Whereas the effect of intra-regional integration on trade is estimated to be rather negligible, stability and the establishment of peace, together with a bigger integrated market, are likely to attract further FDI that will positively influence the catching up process through a pressure to modernisation and adaptation.

In the framework of the neoclassic model, it is often argued that the abolition of trade barriers decreases intra-regional FDI flows, as trade and capital flows are conceived to be substitutable modes of serving foreign markets. However, this negative effect is of minor importance in the Western Balkans: intra-regional FDI flows - apart from Croatian investments in Bosnia and Hercegovina - are not substantial at the moment.

Consequently, a large common market may make the region more attractive for outside foreign investors, especially countries that offer superior location advantages. These countries will be most likely Croatia and, depending on the progress of political and economic reforms, Serbia and Montenegro. It is also possible that the establishment of a FTA generates various dynamic effects that affect FDI flows. An integration process can lead to significant efficiency benefits that may raise the growth rates of participating countries over the medium or long term (Kušić and Zakharov, 2003).

That there is potential for an upraise of FDI flows into the region has been shown empirically by Christie (2003). For Bosnia and Hercegovina, Croatia and Macedonia,[60] he was able to show - using a gravity model that took into account data until 1998 - the region had abnormally low levels of FDI stock, in figures 46.88 per cent of potential inflows. In addition, he could find neither trade substitutability nor complementarity, so that from his study no implications can be drawn on the interplay between FDI and trade in the region.

In fact, a free trade area of 55 million people with access to the markets of the EU, should contribute to improving the image of the region for

---

[60] Due to insufficient or unreliable data, he left out SCG and Albania.

investors and lead to increased private investment within the region and also from outside the region (OECD, 2003).

Yet research has shown that a minimum level of absorptive capacity is necessary to benefit from such transfer (Borensztein and Lee, 1998). Although the Western Balkans may have been better endowed with human capital and skilled labour compared to other low and middle-income countries, this comparative advantage could have been eroded by the war and its consequences, most notably emigration and thus "brain drain". Therefore cooperation in the fields of research and development, human resource management and innovation appears increasingly necessary.

5.3.3.2.3 Infrastructure, Technology, Political Coherence

As South-South integration often is a priori limited by insufficient infrastructure and a lack of coherence in politics, also economic policy, these issues are generally considered promising fields for cooperation. Thus, it is argued that integration enforces cooperation in areas obliquely influencing economic performance. At present, integration may facilitate joint efforts to overcome deficiencies currently limiting the scope of development (Anastasakis and Bojicić-Dželilović, 2002). Many economic problems in the successor states of former SFRJ are regional in nature. Especially in the context of improving infrastructure, cross-national projects need to be promoted that aim at re-building railways, highways, and the communication network (Uvalić, 2000). The main areas of interest will be discussed briefly below.

Infrastructure and Environmental Protection: The energy supply is inadequate, resulting high costs for energy hamper economic recovery. The exclusive concentration on an expansion of energy production on a national level cannot be the solution to the problem. Moreover, intra-regional networks for the supply of power that take into account the extra-regional energy resources should be seriously planned and implemented. What is especially startling in this context are deficits in the environmental sector. Even before the eruption of the war, the region suffered from exuberant pollution as a consequence of decades-long neglect of environmental problems. The conflicts during the nineties completely ousted the problem from the agendas and caused additional problems in the form of direct war damages (Altmann, 2002).

Economic Policy: But not only in the area of environmental economics, also in other areas of politics the developments are partly oppositional. What is attracting attention is the variety in currency issues, especially the side-by-side of EURO and Dinar in Montenegro, which, as a Republic of Serbia and Montenegro, should accept the Dinar as the only legal tender. Different competencies for regulation in all the countries complicate the possibilities for cooperation and limit the free mobility of capital. In general, governmental as well as local authorities have proved to be weak in the past, financial possibilities are limited, corruption and a grey economy are widely spread. In due course, the abolition of trade barriers agreed upon on a state level is not always respected and imposes further barriers on cooperation (Altmann, 2002). In these fields, national policies have to take common measures and create multinational institutions to fight the problem.

Innovation: In addition, the region lags behind in terms of adaptation, application, and improvement of modern technology. Not only commercial structures in the enterprise sector have been disrupted, but also networks in the areas of research, education and innovation. Especially in research and development (R&D), there is huge potential for economies of scale. R&D is a costly input that should be used more efficiently. Today, linkages between universities are only slowly re-emerging, as well as those between research institutions that formerly connected the whole region.

5.4 The Future of Economic Cooperation in the Western Balkans: Chances and Obstacles

The approach of the EU towards the Western Balkans is based on two central assumptions:

1. Cooperation overcomes nationalism and
2. Cooperation has economic advantages.

At present, the only form of cooperation that appears to be sufficiently promoted and that is perceived positively in most cases is integration into the EU. However, wide parts of the population are suffering from the disrupted markets. The free movement of labour has not been granted in the past. The prevailing visa-regimes that only have started vanishing lately not only limit the possibilities for travelling, but also impose restrictions on daily business life. Especially if we assume that a conciliation and cooperation can only be realised through a reanimation of personal contacts on an individual level. In addition, the movement of goods is still barred through formal and informal barriers[61] and slow border controls (Bieber, 2002).

Whereas formally trade barriers as tariffs and quotas will be eliminated, other barriers remain for the moment, most notably poor infrastructure, lengthy and costly payment procedures. Thus, what can be definitely concluded is that institutions and infrastructure should be re-built and developed commonly. In the context of railways, energy, and a reasonable use of existing capacities, especially in the small countries of the Western Balkans there should be given a strong impetus to regional cooperation (Holzner, Christie, and Gligorov, 2004).

From a mere economic viewpoint, it appears somewhat questionable if the EU's approach to the Western Balkans can be justified any longer. The competitiveness of the region is low, so that regional orientation can be seen as an evasive manoeuvre and concluded that the demand for the establishment of a FTA does not promote increasingly competitive production structures.

Cooperation in the Balkans is mainly hindered by political barriers. After the consecutive wars in former SFRJ, a regional cooperation has been nearly unthinkable in the nineties. Thus, in this context, ethnic nationalism is commonly regarded as a main obstacle to cooperation in the Balkans and it is frequently stated that the questions of borders and national identity are an impediment to regional cooperation. Contrarily, they should provide a main incentive to cooperation. Still, the undefined status of Kosovo and Montenegro

---

[61] Passing the borders between Croatia and Republika Srpska may be a drastic example.

and the fragile situation in Bosnia and Hercegovina constitute the major challenges both for the EU and towards regional institutions.

There is a present rhetoric in favour of cooperation, officially, representatives underline their willingness for trans-border cooperation, and however, on-site conversations off records clearly reveal that there are aversions and resistance towards regional cooperation. Obviously, these conditions are the more obvious, the more north-west one moves. The further north the country, the stronger are the ties with and the orientations towards the EU. However, plain talk is not enough. Signing agreements without implementation will not bring the desired results.

Contrarily, on an economic level, the necessity for regional cooperation and – more specifically integration - is seen, and talking to entrepreneurs in the region reveals that there is a will to cooperate and re-vive old distribution channels. Costs of adaptation to other markets are felt to be much lower, old sales channels can more easily be brushed up than new ones opened. Despite the fact that this might be a signal of lacking competitiveness, this also points to the awareness of businesses that old supply channels and capacities need to be enlivened to work efficiently. Enterprises throughout the region feel the pressure for growth and being profitable, so that the North-South incline in terms of readiness for integration that can be felt on a political level does not exist on an economic one (Grupe and Kušić, 2004).

Interestingly, the enterprises of one country that actually is not a part of the Western Balkans but was part of former SFRJ, i.e. Slovenia, are heavily engaged in the whole region, both in terms of trade and FDI. In 2002, Slovenian enterprises had been the second largest investor in Bosnia and Hercegovina (Gama, manufacturing sector) and the fifth largest investor in Serbia (Mercator, retail sector), otherwise only one intra-regional foreign direct investment ranks among the five highest in the respective countries; that was the investment of Finvest Co-Čabar (OECD, 2003); yet more positive tendencies show up.

Thus, will and preparedness for cooperation should strongly be promoted by economic policy. At present, the infrastructure in large parts of the region does not allow for increased exchange. Structures should be created that enable enterprises to turn their will to cooperate into real outcomes. Consequently, non-governmental cooperation in form of civil-society actions has had little effect on the overall climate and performance (Bieber, 2002).

Supporting autonomous initiatives on a business level is especially valuable as it is probable that the region will experience serious costs of delay. The countries of the Western Balkans should not confidently take for granted a repetition of the process in central eastern Europe. Costs of delay manifest themselves even today, and probably will become more and more perceptible if the desired FDI flows will bypass the countries and move further east - to the Asian markets. In addition, also the direct effects of EU integration in financial terms will vanish. EU Funds are successively diminished, and also, the allocation formula will change.

To actively promote these initiatives on a microeconomic level, the establishment of trust and confidence, relations in the business community at large, such as membership in business associations and relations between economic actors and the state are of major importance. Trust, taking an economic viewpoint, is an asset that promotes economic growth by means of lowering transaction costs. Lengthy and costly contracts can be avoided or reduced. Confidence, in contrast, refers to the generalised expectations of how systems operate in a given society. Confidence is thus related to the question of whether or not to enter economic transactions at all, trusts simplifies economic transactions. Whereas confidence is a systemic thing that appeals equally to all participants in the economy, trust is interpersonal, varying from partner to partner (Rus, 2002).

To increase trust among business partners, business associations, fairs and other settings that generate opportunity for contact are helpful. To enhance trust in a country that has very recently experienced the disruption of former united state and was torn by war will be a long-term task, yet can be supported by a legislative environment that provides legal certainty and thus protection. This will promote the establishment of enterprises that are prepared to face the competition with the EU and are willing to share their prospects and difficulties not only within enterprises from their countries, but also with their geographical neighbours. Thus, it may be concluded, cross-border cooperation is most effective when it takes place on a pragmatic and interest-driven level, which excludes national politics.

5.5   Concluding Remarks and Outlook

The analysis has shown that the scope of regional integration for fostering regional trade performance is limited due to similar patterns of specialisation and a dominance of labour-intensive production that offers little room for differentiation. Also an application of the predictions of the new trade theory creates little optimism based on regional integration in terms of the direct effects. Instead of providing a training ground, the alignment to regional markets is unlikely to promote competitiveness but stall microeconomic restructuring.

Yet the increased market size may attract FDI, yielding new knowledge and capital, and the institutional framework provided within the FTA may facilitate cooperation in areas of common interest that currently hamper economic progress. To be able to realise these advantages, the economic sphere needs to be supported by measures taken on a political level to ease economic transactions.

This however is only a credible scenario in the near future if further enforced by the EU, nurturing the conclusion that a successful approach to the EU has to be accompanied through intra-regional integration. The anchor for stability and security and for economic modernisation, however, lies outside the region. Modernisation requires an efficiently huge market and funds of finance. This is not feasible by solely using regional resources. In addition, the prospects for trade are highly dependent on the behaviour of external actors. Thus, the right sequencing of regional integration and EU-integration are important to create sustainable potential for development within the region.

The track record of regional cooperation in terms of the numbers of meetings, declarations, and initiatives is impressive, corruption and environmental pollution are often on the agendas, whereas obvious opportunities for collaboration as free trade, improvement of the infrastructure, and border and visa regulations are only insufficiently emphasised.

However, plain talk is not sufficient, what is needed is cooperation on a basic level between single enterprises and institutions. If trust and confidence will return to the region on all levels, and If this can be displayed credibly to the outside, the perception of the region may change sustainedly. Not only in terms of FDI attraction, but also to forward tourism. This changed perception could enforce economic progress. Local cross border cooperation as well as civil-society networking will eliminate ethnic prejudices and normalise relations.

What is stunning is the inconsistent approach of the European Union to the region: Whereas the EU on one hand makes regional integration a condition for EU accession, it somewhat boosts the lacking political orientation towards regional markets to the benefit of orientation towards the West: instead of integrating the region as a whole, the EU creates new divisions by granting candidate status to distinct countries while having no contracts with others. Then, the EU maintains its individual country approach when dealing with potential applicants. Through this two-sided approach, the region is included in the prospective process of European integration, but excluded form membership for a protracted area of time. The countries of the region fall in different categories of relations with the EU, what they share is that they are all excluded from the benefits of membership.

However, probably this is the only possible approach: The EU combines support with pressure to restructuring. To make the region succeed economically, it requires parallel North-South and South-South integration. Only through this proceeding, the danger of one-sided specialisation can be banned. If the EU would only take a regional approach, the effects of increased regional integration might even be negative in terms of microeconomic restructuring. In addition, simply waiting for the EU to approach them will not suffice the countries of the region. Moreover, independent restructuring and specialisation are required.

Today, European integration has become the shared ideal for individuals, communities, and states in the Western Balkans and thus unites the region. To achieve the aim, and to overcome structural deficits and recent legacies of war and conflict, a functioning of states and the demonstrated willingness for cooperation are a conditio sine qua non. Often, regional integration in the regional perception is understood as a sidetrack for the postponement of integration. However, regional integration goes beyond being a precondition for EU integration in unfolding its value for prosperity and stability.

Bibliography

ALTMANN, F.-L. (2002): Regionale Kooperation in Südosteuropa – Organisationen, Pläne, Erfahrungen, Balkan Forum: regionale Kooperation und europäische Integration des Westbalkans.

ANASTASAKIS, O., AND BOJICIĆ-DŽELILOVIĆ, V. (2002): Balkan Regional Cooperation & European Integration, The Hellenic Observatory, London School of Economics.

BALASSA, B. (1965): Trade Liberalization and "Revealed" Comparative Advantage, The Manchester School, (33), 99–123.

BALASSA, B. (1989): Comparative Advantage, Trade Policy and Economic Development, New York.

BARTLETT, W., AND BUKVIČ, V. (2002): What are the Main Barriers to SME Growth and Development in South East Europe? In Small Enterprise Development in South East Europe. Policies for Sustainable Growth, ed. by W. Bartlett, M. Bateman, and M. Vehovec, pp. 17–37. Kluwer Academic Publishers, Dordrecht.

BIEBER, F. (2002): Bi- und multinationale politische Kooperation auf dem Westbalkan, Balkan Forum Regionale Kooperation und europäische Integration des Westbalkans.

BLOMSTROM, M., AND KOKKO, A. (1997): How Foreign Investment Affects Host Countries, World Bank Policy Research Working Paper 1745.

BORENSZTEIN, E., DE GREGORIO, J., AND LEE, J.-W. (1998): How Does Foreign Direct Investment Affect Economic Growth? Journal of International Econo-mics, 45(1), pp. 115–135.

CHRISTIE, E. (2002): Potential Trade in Southeast Europe: a Gravity Model Approach, wiiw Working Papers, (21).

CHRISTIE, E. (2003): Foreign Direct Investment in Southeast Europe, wiiw Working Papers, (24).

DUNNING, J. (1993): Multinational Enterprises and the Global Economy Workplan, Addison-Wesley, Berkshire.

EUROPEAN ECONOMY. EUROPEAN COMMISSION, DIRECTORATE-GENERAL FOR ECONOMIC AND FINANCIAL AFFAIRS (2004): The Western Balkans in Transition, Directorate-General for Economic and Financial Affairs.

GAUČAITĖ WITTICH, V. (2005): Some Aspects of Recent Trade Developments in South-East Europe, UNECE Discussion Paper Series No. 7, December 2005, Geneva.

GLIGOROV, V. (1998): Trade and Investments in the Balkans, in: On the Way to Normality, The States on the Territory of Former Yugoslavia in the Postwar Period, ed. by V. Gligorov, and H. Vidovic, pp. 1–24. WIIW Research Report No. 250, Vienna Institute for International Economic Studies, Vienna.

GLIGOROV, V. (2004): The Economic Development in Southeast Europe after 1999/2000, Südosteuropa Mitteilungen. Special Issue: Five Years of Stability Pact. Regional Cooperation in Southeast Europe.

GRUPE, C., AND KUŠIĆ, S. (2004): Is Croatia Prepared to Join the EU in 2007? Building Competitive Advantage, Paper presented at the 8th EACES Conference in Belgrade.

HOLZNER, M., CHRISTIE, E., AND GLIGOROV, V. (2004): Infrastructural Needs & Economic Development in South-Eastern Europe. The Case of Rail and Road Transport Infrastructure" Functional Borders and Sustainable Security: Integrating the Balkans in the European Union, IBEU, (4).

HORN, A., AND KUŠIĆ, S. (2001): Chancen einer Exportorientierten Entwicklungsstrategie für Albanien, Südosteuropa Mitteilungen, 41(1), pp. 50–61.

KAMINSKI, B., AND DE LA ROCHA, M. (2003): Stabilization and Association Process in the Balkans: Integration Options and their Assessment, World Bank Policy Research Working Paper 3108.

KRUGMAN, P. R., AND OBSTFELD, M. (2003): International Economics. Theory and Policy, Addison-Wesley World Student Series, Boston, 6 edn.

KUŠIĆ, S. (2002): Gewinner und Verlierer der Transformation: System- und länderspezifische Ausgangsbedingungen, alternative Transformationspfade und EU Integration, Gewinner und Verlierer der postsozialistischer Transformationsprozesse; 10. Brühler Tagung junger Osteuropa-Experten Deutsche Gesellschaft für Osteuropakunde; Forschungsstelle Osteuropa Bremen Arbeitspapiere und Materialien, (36), pp. 11–15.

KUŠIĆ, S., AND GRUPE, C. (2004): Über die Wettbewerbsfähigkeit – Definitionsversuche und Erklärungsansätze, Ekonomski pregled, Zagreb, 55(9-10), pp. 804–814.

KUŠIĆ, S., AND ZAKHAROV, V. (2003): The Role of FDI in the EU Accession Process: The Case of the Western Balkans, Conference papers, European Trade Study Group (ETSG), September 2003, Madrid.

OECD (2002): Progress in Policy Reform in South East Europe. Monitoring Instruments, OECD. Stability Pact. South East Europe Compact for Reform, Investment, Integrity and Growth.

OECD (2003): Progress in Policy Reform in South East Europe. Monitoring Instruments, OECD. Stability Pact. South East Europe Compact for Reform, Investment, Integrity and Growth.

ROBSON, P. (1998): The Economics of International Integration, London, 4 edn.

ROGGEMANN, H. (1970): Das Modell der Arbeiterselbstverwaltung in Jugoslawien. Europäische Verlagsgesellschaft, Frankfurt am Main.

RUS, A. (2002): Social Capital and SME Development, in: Small Enterprise Development in South East Europe. Policies for Sustainable Growth, ed. by W. Bartlett, M. Bateman, and M. Vehovec, pp. 39–69. Kluwer Academic Publishers, Dordrecht.

SANFEY, P., FALCETTI, E., TACI, A., AND TEPIĆ, S. (2004): Spotlight on South Eastern Europe. An overview of private sector activity and investment, EBRD.

SHLEIFER, A., AND VISHNY, R. (1993): Corruption, NBER Working Papers, (4372).

UNCTAD (2002): Improving the Competitiveness of SMEs through Enhancing Productive Capacity, UNCTAD Trade and Development Board. Commission on Enterprise, Business Facilitation and Development.

UVALIĆ, M. (1993): The Disintegration of Yugoslavia: Its costs and benefits, Communist Economies and Economic Transformation, 5(3), 273–293.

UVALIĆ, M. (2000): Regional Cooperation and Economic Integration in South Eastern Europe, Paper presented at the 6th EACES Conference in Barcelona, 7-9 September 2000.

VENABLES, A. J. (1987): Customs Union, Tariff Reform and Imperfect Competition, European Economic Review, (31), pp. 103–110.

VINER, J. (1950): The Customs Union Issue. Carnegie Endowment for International Peace, New York.

VLAHINIĆ-DIZDAREVIĆ, N., AND KUŠIĆ, S. (2004): Regional Trade Agreement in Southeast Europe: a Force for Convergence? Conference proceedings, International Symposium "Economics and Management of Trans-formation" (ed.) University of the West, Timisoara – Faculty of Economic Sciences Timisoara, Romania.

VON HAGEN, J., AND TRAISTARU, I. (2003): The South East Europe Review 2002-2003, World Economic Forum.

WALZ, U. (1999): Dynamics of Regional Integration. Physica-Verlag, Heidelberg.

Contributors

Paulina Biernacka. Ph.D Student at Warsaw University, Poland.

PD Dr. Daniel Göler. Institut for Geography, University of Bamberg, Germany.

Claudia Grupe. Ph.D Student at Johann Wolfgang Goethe-University Frankfurt, Germany.

M.A.Vedran Horvat. Head of Heinrich Böll Foundation Zagreb, Croatia.

Dr. Siniša Kušić. Faculty of Economics and Business Administration, Johann Wolfgang Goethe-University Frankfurt, Germany.

Isa Mulaj. Ph.D Student at Staffordshire University, United Kingdom, Integra Consulting, and Institute for Economic Policy Research and Analysis (INEPRA), Prishtina.

Siniša Kušić (ed.)

Path-Dependent Development in the Western Balkans
The Impact of Privatization

Frankfurt am Main, Berlin, Bern, Bruxelles, New York, Oxford, Wien, 2005.
220 pp., num. tab., 1 graf.
ISBN-10: 3-631-53581-3 / ISBN-13: 978-3-631-53581-3
US-ISBN: 978-0-8204-7692-6 · pb. € 39.–*

Despite of structural commonalities resulting from the shared socialist heritage, regional, historical, and cultural peculiarities of every country place a crucial impact on shape and speed of post-socialist development. This applies especially to the process of privatization in transition; methods were chosen to bring in line the socialist legacies and the demands of a fast and as painless as possible transition to a market economy. The compendium aims at accessing choice and success of privatization methods in the Western Balkans with regard to the countries' attributes. The impacts of privatization on enterprise performance and efficiency, private entrepreneurship, competitiveness, the role of the state, and macroeconomic data in the countries of the Western Balkans are related to the countries' distinct features. In six contributions experts from the region analyze these interdependencies in detail.

Contents: Siniša Kušić: Path-dependency in the Process of Privatization · *Claudia Grupe*: The Western Balkans: Past – Present – Future · *Domagoj Račić / Vladimir Cvijanović*: Privatization, Institution Building and Market Development: The Case of Croatia · *Dragoljub Stojanov / Claudia Grupe*: BiH Privatization and Workers' Participation as an Example of Economic Robbery – A Case Study of "Agrokomerc" · *Milorad Filipović / Miroljub Hadžić*: Serbian Privatization – From Social Toward Private Ownership and From Self-Management Toward Proper Governing · *Isa Mulaj*: Delayed Privatization in Kosovo: Causes, Consequences, and Implications in the Ongoing Process · *Saso Arsov*: Post-Privatization Retrospective of Macedonia: Could We Have Done It Better? · *Fatmir Mema / Ines Dika*: Privatization and Post-Privatization in Albania: A Long and Difficult Path

Frankfurt am Main · Berlin · Bern · Bruxelles · New York · Oxford · Wien
Distribution: Verlag Peter Lang AG
Moosstr. 1, CH-2542 Pieterlen
Telefax 00 41 (0) 32 / 376 17 27

*The €-price includes German tax rate
Prices are subject to change without notice
Homepage http://www.peterlang.de

Peter Lang · Europäischer Verlag der Wissenschaften